SLIGHTLY
SKEWED
VIGNETTES

CONFESSIONS OF AN INCORRIGIBLE KID

K a r l R o h n k e

KENDALL/HUNT PUBLISHING COMPANY
2460 Kerper Boulevard P.O. Box 539 Dubuque, Iowa 52004-0539

This book is dedicated to the memory of my mother:
Gladys Kutcher Rohnke

Gratuities

I've learned that writing a book, even if your name is listed as sole author, isn't a completely solitary task. I've received help with this collection of stories from a number of people and they are:

Bonnie Hannable proofread the manuscript and said nice things about what she read.

The people who have joined me in these adventures, particularly *John Herbert*, a most adventurous friend.

Gloree Rohnke, who knows me well and has provided me with valuable insights into my writing and myself.

Plynn Williams, who once again has utilized his cartooning skills and offbeat sense of humor to capture the skewed essence of these often bizarre adventures.

Project Adventure, generically, for providing the conceptual and physical testing ground that has resulted in many currently used curriculum classics, and the occasional vignette, a few of which have made it into this anthology.

If you would like to know more about this adventurous company, write to: **Project Adventure, Inc., P.O. Box 100, Hamilton, MA 01936** and ask for ". . . all the free stuff you can send me."

Table of Contents

Introduction

"Find out what you don't do well, then don't do it."

"ALF"

I was filling out a form the other day (tax return actually), and one of the blank spaces asked for my occupation. . . I hesitated. In the past if someone asked me what I did for a living, I would answer, *teacher*, and that was the end of that. *Teacher* is a perfect response if you don't want to answer questions about , "what you do . . ." because everyone knows that a teacher teaches. Even if someone, to be polite, asks what I teach, I simply say biology or social studies, or English . . . and that *is* the end of that. Anyway, this time I filled in the blank space with the wishful appellation—*writer*, because there was nobody there to ask me, "Write what?"

For a number of years I have earned part of my living as a how-to writer, specializing in expository text of: how to play games, how to lead initiative problems, tie knots, build ropes courses, etc. During that time I have consciously tried to embellish a writing style that emphasizes tongue-in-cheek humor, a benign irreverence for the subject, and an occasional disregard for grammar and proper vocabulary. People occasionally tell me that they appreciate the way I have tried to make potentially tedious material fun to read, and that has been my criteria for success; fun first, then leave some room for learning.

Vignettes offers no lessons, and has no hidden agenda. I'm sure you could find a worthwhile message or two within the stories (don't do this, and don't do that . . .), but my purpose in recording and writing about these poignant slices of life was purely selfish, I enjoyed doing it.

The Tower was the first article I recorded for this anthology of TRUE stories, and that was about two years ago. Some of the tales actually occurred long ago (I was fifteen when *Kitchen Capers* took place), but what happened on that day isn't something you forget—ever. I checked the story line with my Mom, and she verified the facts; mothers don't forget.

As emphasized in the paragraph above, *ALL* these stories are true—save one. Did you ever play the game, *Two Truths and a Lie?*

Well, this book represents seventeen truths and a lie. The only reason I'm admitting to one fictional foray is to increase the fun I hope you'll have perusing these slightly skewed escapades. Which story do you think is apocryphal? It's not *Kitchen Capers*!

Some of the vignettes in this collection make me cringe when I think about the potentials for disaster, but that's what makes them an interesting read. Each story has a twist or two that makes it unique and down-to-earth different from the hair-shirt, world-class, elitist adventures of the *Outside Magazine* genre. If the .50 caliber slugs had not exploded on the stove, the story about lead collecting in *Kitchen Capers* was mildly interesting, but hardly worth including. Darting pigeons with a blowgun is no more than a culling interlude until the cherry bomb adaptation produces a surprise escalation to the pigeon control plan. "Bad things" could have happened to me during these escapades but those "things" didn't happen, and I'm still here to gently strain off the angst and embellish the humor.

Rationale - Why I Still Do What I Used To Do

"I looked up and saw a squirrel jump from one high tree to another. He appeared to be aiming for a limb so far out of reach that the leap looked like suicide. He missed - but landed, safe and unconcerned, on the branch several feet lower. Then he climbed to his goal and all was well.

Since then whenever I have to choose between risking a new venture or hanging back, I remember those crazy air-borne squirrels and think, 'They've got to risk it if they don't want to spend the rest of their lives in one tree'.

So, I've jumped again and again. And in jumping, I've learned why the squirrels so often do it; it's fun."

Oscar Schisgall

I have never gone out of my way back then, or more recently, to purposefully place myself in compromising or dangerous situations for the sake of "living on the edge." However, I have always been on the lookout for adventure, and by definition adventurous situations are associated with risk. Like most kids and many adults, I have taken some unreasonable risks, but this resulted from kinetic curiosity, or responding to the challenge of going farther, higher, faster or deeper, and were not emotionally unhealthy risks. But I'm not a kid anymore (although I try), so the situations I have written about that have taken place in the

last five years or so (*OZ Waters*, *Rock Running*, *3–2-1 Bungee* and others), are simply the result of what I like to think of as a healthy desire to do more than drink Coke and watch *The Gladiators* on TV.

In order to maximize whatever hormonal tweak the stories initiate, pick a chapter title at random and read it when you have the time to let your imagination experientially join me as an existential participant (sorry, there's no accompanying video, or follow up text). And, for your convenience, please note that I have kept the stories brief for those of you who read best on the bidet . . . or whatever you happen to be sitting on. Adventure is where you find it!

Be careful most of the time. Stay healthy. Have some fun.

CHAPTER 1

Kitchen Capers

"Game over man! Game Over!"
Pvt. Hudson—The movie ALIENS

I've always liked the metal lead. I like the heaviness and the heft, but, as attractively inertial as the metal is, it's also vulnerable (like gold)—easy to scratch and easy to melt.

In 1952, I was fifteen years old and living with my parents in Kailua township on the windward side of Oahu, Hawaii, then still a territory of the United States. At fifteen, like all teenagers, I needed spending money, and jobs were hard to come by. I had worked for a few weeks on a dairy farm spreading manure on a hillside for $.75 per hour—not bad at the time, considering that I was only getting $.25 an hour for baby-sitting. But I wanted some REAL money, and *lead* proved to be my fool's gold.

Kaneohe Marine air station was located about five miles from my Ohana street home. Part of that military base (which I had access to, since my dad was a career officer in the Coast Guard) was Fort Hase, located on a scrub-covered peninsula, with hills that descended sharply to the rugged coral and lava coast. Over the millennia, ocean waves had worn away at this igneous shore interface causing an abrupt and precipitous juxtaposing twixt water and land. If you wanted to snorkel beyond the shore break, you had to leap into the surf with diving gear in hand just at the very moment a large swell provided the vehicle to carry you away from the sharp coral. Exciting to think about now, just necessary back then.

The guys that I hung around with after school were avid divers and surfers. On weekends and during the summers, we would occasionally run, walk, or hitch down to Fort Hase's restricted area to explore the abandoned but still intact World War 11, sixteen-inch gun implacements, and amuse ourselves amongst the tangle of combat trash (treasure to any 15-year-old that loved helmets, hand grenade shells, slightly bent propellers, and machine guns.)

I have to tell you something as an aside, and I guess it's OK considering that all this stuff I'm writing about took place almost 40 years ago. Amongst the military junk and outdated killing gear, half-buried under various plane parts, I found a wing-mount .50 caliber air cooled machine gun. What a find! What a treasure! Can you imagine what it was like to be fifteen and find something so extrinsically worthless, yet beyond value? It must have weighed 30+ pounds, and I still can't remember how I transported it the five miles to

2

my house. Such joy, even now, just to write this and remember the poignancy of that find.

We also did quite a bit of spear fishing directly off the reef. On more than one occasion we came ashore with a few bagged lobsters, started a fire near the shore line, and boiled up the "bugs" for lunch in one of the steel G.I. Joe-type helmets. No butter, but no complaints.

On one predictably beautiful Polynesian day, as shooting fish and plucking lobster paled, I noticed, peppered on the alternating sand/coral bottom, literally hundreds of lead sinkers that had been lost over the years by shore casting fisherman. There were also hundreds of hooks, swivels, and lures attached to untold and Gordienly-tangled meters of fishing line. Remember, this was the early 50's, and sport diving was still in its infancy: the invention of the aqua lung by Jacques Cousteau had occurred only eight years earlier. Even though this location provided ideal visibility and many fish, access was limited by the military and the difficult water entry. No one knew of this treasure trove, except what the native fishermen knew intuitively, and they were strictly land casters.

The "ulua" hooks and swivels were our immediate commercial targets. They were easy to retrieve off the bottom and light enough to preclude struggling with in the water. We brought the collected gear ashore, scraped off the stinky marine growth, and tried to sell the rejuvenated tackle to the fisherman. I suspect it was sour grapes on their part, considering that we continued plucking lead off the bottom while they were fishing, but the locals (*kanakas*) didn't want to buy used fishing gear from young *haoles* (Caucasians) that probably belonged to them in the first place. Most of my buddies left it at that, and returned to spearing hapless *maninis* (a small striped fish that was slow and fatally curious). I returned for the *lead*.

One of my non-diving friends was a dedicated "mauser" (someone who loves to root around in dumps) and he mentioned to me that lead was fetching a good price on the scrap market; $.14 a pound as I remember. Considering that I had a practically unlimited supply of this "precious" metal lying at a depth of 10–30 feet on the ocean floor, a light bulb went off and I was consumed by entrepreneurial visions of cornering the lead market.

If you have ever done any SCUBA diving (almost unheard of in the early 50's) you know that a lead weight belt is necessary to adjust the diver's buoyancy. If the belt is too light, it's hard for a diver to stay down, and if too heavy, the diver struggles to keep off the bottom. I was practically pinned to the bottom after about five minutes of plucking sinkers. Experiencing a one-mindedness about my collecting task that bordered on suicidal, I collected lead off the sea bottom until

3

my self-imposed anchor was practically impossible to move, but I moved it by walking on the bottom, convinced that my fortune was being made. I became very fit during this time period and very water-logged.

The sinkers were usually covered with marine growth, so the fishermen showed little interest in my treasure. During this time, I transported untold heavy loads the five miles to my home via bicycle trips. (I would have never completed those heavily laden trips on a 10 speed bike. Single-speed, balloon-tire bikes were the transportation of choice for young teens back then.)

My friends thought I had flipped, so they ignored my frantic collecting efforts. My mother knew I did funny things, so she didn't say much, and my father (a career Coast Guard officer) was at sea: perfect. I was the sole owner of *Rohnke's Lead Ingot Company*.

The scrap company that was willing to pay 14 cents a pound for my deep-six treasure didn't want a bunch of smelly, algae-covered, chunks of lead; they wanted shiny ingots of the pure stuff. My greed knew no bounds as I fired up the stoves of entreprenurial intent—actually just my mom's gas kitchen stove burner.

When my mother left the house, the lead-melting began. I wasn't being purposefully sneaky, just understanding of predictable parental negativism, and lack of entrepreneurial perspicacity by adult types over twenty years old.

I had a perfect rectangular container for melting the lead, and it coincidentally fit ideally on the kitchen burner. Have you ever melted lead? It's great fun. When the melting point is reached, all the impurities rise to the surface as the pure and shiny liquid lead wobbles kinetically beneath the glop. When you pour off the essence, the end product (before it cools) looks like gleaming silver. But I think the part that appealed most was the borderline control of a dangerous material as it pertained to the obvious potential for disaster. Knowing that this beautiful flowing silver substance could and would destroy any burnable substance it touched i.e., me, made the whole melting/pouring scenario exciting.

I made a few ingots successfully, and somewhat reluctantly sold them for an agreed-upon price. After going to all the trouble of collecting the lead, transporting it, cleaning it, and melting it, I became possessive of those stacked ingots. But, money being what it is, I succumbed to the crisp green for the heavy silver.

I suppose this would have been the end of the story, if I had not discovered the machine gun target range at Fort Hase. As part of our teenage perambulations, in areas where we probably shouldn't have been, we came upon a set of railroad tracks that didn't seem to go anywhere, just in an oval, like a Lionel train set. As we explored the area, we found a small electric-powered train car that pulled what looked like a small flatbed with pocked and shredded canvas targets on it. Both the electric car and the flatbed were heavily armored. As it turned out, this was a .50 caliber machine gun target range. The practicing gunners tried to hit the moving train targets from a considerable distance away; over 1,000 meters (we paced it off). The area behind the tracks displayed a bull-dozed dirt hill about 10 meters high, to stop errant .50 caliber slugs. A couple hundred meters beyond the dirt hill was the ocean, the ultimate backstop.

We happily poked around the area, trying to reconstruct what the pounding slugs must have done to the targets, and just enjoying the benign aura of past war exploits. Somebody walked over to the hill, dug around a bit, and shouted, "There's thousands of them here." We all ran over, and indeed there were, .50 caliber slugs on the surface, half-buried, smooshed, smashed—everywhere. Picking them up and throwing them around was fun, but the throwing stopped when I realized that each slug was made up of copper with a LEAD filling. There was hundreds of pounds of lead just lying around on the ground—I DIDN'T EVEN HAVE TO DIVE FOR IT. I was once again seized with lead mania. My bicycle trips to Fort Hase increased, but I was truckin' a different load.

A friend of mine from Kailua Intermediate School, Wilfred Silva, was fascinated by my entrepreneurial spirit (he needed money, too) and had helped me in the past with my melting efforts. I gave him a comparatively small percentage of the profits, mostly because he was younger and smaller than me, but also because he didn't do any of the diving or transporting. It was more or less a fair deal.

I don't remember the day or even the month that the explosion occurred, but the events of that day are etched indelibly in my memory: I missed death or disfigurement by seconds.

Wilfred and I loaded up the melting canister on that day with about five pounds of sinker lead. (My mother was shopping.) Our kitchen stove (gas) took about five minutes to start the lead liquifying. When I noticed the shifting/compacting movement of the sinkers that indicated the melting point had been reached, I *carefully* dipped half a dozen .50 caliber slugs into the quaking silver. I watched them curiously, my face inches above the container, waiting for the lead interior of the slugs to liquify and join the melted mass. It occurred to me that when this happened I would need a pair of pliers to remove the unmelted copper exterior of the bullet, so I walked to my room where I had last seen the pliers. Wilfred was on the far side of the kitchen at the sink scrubbing sinkers when I left the room.

5

I was on my way back to the kitchen when I heard the explosion, then immediately a scream. I entered the room with trepidation and (this is hard to admit) curiosity. My mind had trouble recording what I saw, I didn't want to believe the mess. The top of the stove was coated in steaming silver. The walls were splotched with smoking silver. The linoleum directly beneath the stove was solid smokin' silver, and there were holes in things that should have been solid, including Wilfred's shirt. Wilfred was still yelling and grasping at his back, his fingers catching in the pock-marked remains of his Aloha shirt.

My reaction was typically teenager—"Oh boy, I'm in **BIG** trouble." Then I thought, ". . . maybe I better do something about Wilfred." His screaming was definitely getting my attention.

When the explosive tracer head of the machine gun slug had exploded (Ed note: I had better explain this bit of pyrotechnics to those of you who have no experience with heavy caliber ordnance. I sure didn't know . . . When a .50 caliber machine gun is being fired, the slugs come out of the barrel at a tremendous rate. To help the gunner adjust his aim, every fifth slug has a tracer head built into it; i.e., a powder charge on the tip of the slug that is ignited by the friction heat of its flight. So as the slugs pour out of the barrel, a steady arcing stream of incendiary lights indicate where the rounds are headed.) Wilfred was fortunately about 15 feet away, so only small blobs of molten lead reached his back, but the flying lead was still hot enough to burn through his shirt and pepper his back with burn blisters. He was hysterical, so I told him to go home. He ran out the back kitchen door, screaming that I would have to pay for his shirt; I never did.

As I started to clean up the kitchen I noticed that a piece of shrapnel had gone through the ceiling directly above the canister. The stove was a disaster, and what was left of the linoleum floor was unsalvageable. I did get most of the splattered lead off the walls, at least to my satisfaction. Having put in the best part of an hour cleaning up, I reckoned that I deserved a break, so I headed for the beach, which was only a block away. I remained there (a couple hours) until my mother showed up looking for me. By that time, the disaster had faded to an inconvenience, and I couldn't understand why she was so upset, particularly since I had gone to such trouble scraping lead off everything. However she was. . . upset. I still think Wilfred's mother had a lot to do with it.

My grandparents were visiting at the time, so granddad got the task of being the heavy, since my dad was still at sea. He laid on the skreed of typical adult indignation, which I politely accepted and promptly forgot. Grandad also went up into the attic and retrieved the shrapnel that was imbedded in a roof joist. I began to appreciate the potential of what might have happened, as it was pointed out what this jagged piece of metal would have done to my face, not to mention the pounds of molten lead that splattered the walls. I became as contrite as an immortal teenager can be.

About six weeks later, I was again in need of some pocket change, and there was a load of sinkers left in the garage. I knew enough by this time not to mess with explosives again, and I only had about 20 pounds of lead to melt down—then I'd be done for good. The explosion had destroyed my good melting cannister (among other things), so I looked around the garage and found a metal container that was about the same size. When my Mom went out (Grandparents had returned to the states), I fired up the new stove and plopped the container on the flames. I had not had the opportunity to take chemistry in high school yet, so my knowledge of melting points was limited to lead: I had no idea that aluminum had such a low melting point.

After the lead had melted, I tried to pick up the now oddly-shaped container with a pair of pliers to pour the molten lead into an ingot mold. The putty-like aluminum sides of the container folded as the bottom fell out. The hot dense liquid, obeying the immutable laws of gravity, flowed predictably toward the center of the earth, but as luck would have it, the *new* linoleum floor happened to be in the way.

The next week, when my Mom went out, I was still at the house, having been grounded for an indefinite length of time, but I had a companion; Mrs. Inoye—my babysitter.

CHAPTER 2

The Pigeon Contract

*"I'm still crazy as hell, but if I don't
drink or use drugs, nobody will notice."*
Recovering Mental Patient

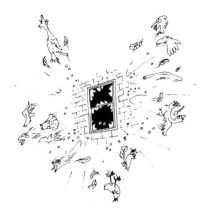

I was a college freshman when I got hold of my first real blow gun. I'm not sure where it came from, but I have a sneaking suspicion that my parents didn't give it to me.

You know how it is sometimes when you have an initial feel for something. You pick it up and *know* that you are going to like it and be good at whatever there is to be good at. That's what it was like with the blowgun; I liked its simplistic look and feel, and was blown away (heh, heh) with the accuracy and power of such a basic weapon. I still have that original anodized tube-with-a-mouthpiece packed away somewhere.

Since then I have picked up a couple similar models that were longer, more powerful, and intrinsically more accurate, but the essential propulsion and bifocal (both eyes open) aiming procedure were the same. The dart comes in one of two styles that I know of—a plastic ball (sized to the diameter of the tube) with a 3" long metal wire dart shaft that you melt into the ball, and a plastic cone which also sports an identical melted-in wire dart. The cone shape is more aerodynamic and therefore packs more of a punch. The *punch* will drive an *unsharp*-ened dart through a piece of 1/4" plywood at thirty feet; this is no toy.

Following a compulsive pattern of overdoing whatever I'm currently interested in, I practiced blowing darts to excess, most of the time at paper targets, but occasionally at lizards and snakes while stationed at Ft. Sam Houston in Texas. But the highlight (lowlight) of my blowgun career was the occasion that I hired on as an oral hit man for a Greek fraternity at the university I was attending.

The fraternity, of which I was a some time member, (*clarification*—joining a frat is supposed to be for life—blood brothers, secret hand shake, and all that—but I joined for a place to eat and sleep and kept my fraternal counsel with chosen friends rather than institutionalized "brothers.") All in all, however, not a bad place to spend four years.

The "brothers" had established an on going territorial war with the local pigeon population. There was a Baptist church directly across the street from the frat house whose belfry acted as a pigeon breeding area, and since that eyrie was sacrosanct (no .22 sniper shots allowed) verily the birds begat in abundance and were a scourge upon the earth, and particularly upon the flat roof just outside the upstairs bathroom that we used for suntanning. Pigeon *doo doo* has no redeeming value or place in a sun tanning area, in addition the constant cooing of the preening males, surfeit with testosterone, was enough to result in a few institutionally incisive comments aimed at their demise. Enter the hit man.

For a small fee, I was willing to stake out the rooftop and mortally dart a few of the offending birds in hopes that this overt display of aggression would cause the remaining flock to flee—permanently. So I staked out the roof and wind-shot the dominant males with my trusty blow gun, performing such a sneaky and silent job that the rest of the dumb birds didn't even know they were being decimated. I suppose I could have continued my clandestine slaughter, but the effectiveness of achieving zero sum pigeons was minimal, and I was losing an inordinate number of darts. I also think they were hatching them out at the church faster than I could get rid of them.

But I was dedicated to my task, as only a college student with nothing else to do but study could be. It was at this frustrating juncture, certain that the brothers would have the last laugh, and fearing that the bonus I had been promised was slipping away, I had the idea which was to soon enshrine me in the avian population control hall of fame.

For the next couple days, rather than darting pigeons, I fed them, and fed them prodigiously, spreading vast quantities of Wonder Bread on the roof top. Never had there been so many cooing and gobbling pigeons in such a small area. Each time I spread a loaf, their crisscrossing flight and glide paths caused considerable rooftop skidding and tumbling over each other in their haste to gobble the feast. With the increase of food came the biologically predictable and very visible increase in cloacal/fecal action. If my plan didn't work, I was in proverbial deep doo doo.

Cherry bombs were easy to come by in the South in the 50's. These round, red, and extremely powerful firecrackers were frequently set off inside and outside the fraternities, and at various athletic events. I had free access to enough cherry bombs to do really bad things, but in this case their utilization toward a final population solution was purely mercenary, albeit slightly skewed toward fraternal altruism.

Continuing my plan, I searched around the frat house looking for an old or unused length of electrical wiring. The lamp I found in the basement was kind of new but I appropriated the wire because I was on a quest (it was Sunday—the hardware store was closed). I separated the ends of the wire and stripped the rubber insulation from the split ends, then spliced the two exposed copper wires together. There was, of course, a regular two-prong plug on the other end of the wire. Then I carefully pulled the fuse out of a cherry bomb and inserted the spliced wires, through the fuse gap hole I had just created, into the round body of the bomb itself. Using some Duco airplane cement, I filled the hole with goo, essentially gluing the wire to the bomb. Using the same tube of glue, I squeezed a copious amount of the clear adhesive all over the exterior of the "cherry," then rolled the sticky red ball in BB's (you know, the copper Red Rider kind). Duco cement dries quickly, smells funny too. I was ready to rock and roll.

It was late afternoon and just about feeding time. Most of the brothers were either studying at the library or were away for the weekend: pyrotechnic perfection. Garnishing the roof with double the amount of Wonder Bread (I hate Wonder Bread), I placed my BB-cluster, pigeon exterminator amidst the manna. The pigeons, perched on nearby tree limbs, looked like vultures just waiting, waiting to gobble that white styrofoam-like bread. I climbed back through the single dormer window into the bathroom amidst much fluttering and cooing, and lowered myself to the floor.

The bottom of the window was just about flush with the roof. Inside, the sill of the window was about at chest height, so that I could easily see the wild eating frenzy taking place. Ducking down and thinking "Make my day!", (even though Clint Eastwood hadn't even portrayed Rowdy Yates yet), I picked up the wire plug and purposefully inserted the double prongs into the wall receptacle.

KA—BLAM!!!

and then instantaneously

CRASH!! TINKLE! TINKLE! TINKLE tinkle

The carnage was nouveau abattoir, and the bathroom floor was covered with glass: pinkish feathers floated lazily everywhere. WOW! I was impressed. The blast finished off every rectangular piece of glass in the window frame. I couldn't believe I had forgotten the window. But that could be fixed—and look at the pigeons . . . there weren't any—still moving. My victory was complete. I noticed red splotches on my arms and wondered vaguely if it was me or the pigeons.

As the result of this innovative culling operation, the common cherry bomb was now looked upon by the administration with a more paternal, yea restrictive eye, and I was looked at by my fraternity brothers with a combination of awe and the distancing respect that is afforded those who's drummer is slightly off center. As time went by (I was only a freshman) the incident became just another crazy interlude that happens occasionally in a college frat environment, and I was socially elevated from avoidable, to nicely nuts—not a bad modus operandi at the time.

A week later, the pigeons were back in force, and I recognized and yielded to the ultimate futility of battling nature and the Baptist church.

CHAPTER 3

Wrongs of Passage

"The difference between genius and
stupidity is that genius has its limits."

Anonymous

College in the late 50's, was . . . college in the late 50's. Now anything associated with the 50's has become a golden oldie, which I guess is typical of all non-war, minimum social protest times in our past. But I remember something particularly distasteful from those *golden* days. . . .

In 1956 I was enrolled as a freshman at a university in the South. The memory that seems most vivid during those first few impressionable days of academia wasn't academic, geographic, sexual, or social, it was being rushed. *Rushed*, what a perfectly descriptive term to relate what the fraternities do to those socially quivering, inexperienced, trusting, fuzzy-cheeked, beer receptacles.

Overdressed in tweed coat and striped tie, I slouched nervously on my saggy-spring dorm bed wondering *why*. . . . Glancing out the third floor window, my attention drawn to the quadrangle below by the increasing hubbub of collecting voices, I saw what looked like a runner's finish tape separating the open end of the quad from the surrounding grass and concrete sidewalks. Behind that tautly-stretched, quivering yellow strip of plastic were the growing sounds of an eager army, a shifting, jostling, impeccably dressed sea of *Greek Letter Fraternity Men*. A sudden and irrational fear manifested itself; they were all going to race up the stairs to *my* room and . . . Ridiculous! They're no more interested in me than . . . **BANG!** A gunshot? Someone fired a starting gun. What's this, a competition? That sartorial sea of tweedy sport coats and rep ties were surging, no . . . running toward the stairwells. I could hear their penny loafers booming on the stairs, hall doors

slamming, excited shouts . . . knock, knock, knock, knock, bam. . .

blam . . . SLAM! Hello Skip?* I'm Biff Knickerbocker representing the best fraternity on campus. What a rat race, eh? Say Skip, I like your tie, nice choice. Skip, you know why I'm here; can I be candid? (No break for an answer.) How about joining us (Kappa Sigma Something) tomorrow over at *the house*, so you can get to meet some of the brothers? We'll relax, pop a few, shoot the bull, and . . . we're having a few *women* join us from Sweet Briar down the road. Whatta ya say, Skip? Tomorrow at 10:00? Great! . . . See you then Skip. Bring that tie! (forced laugh) SLAM! *Hey Mongo!* Who's next on this floor?

---

*I used to be known as Skip, until Karl took over.

So, on the following day, notwithstanding rampant misgivings, I gave way to the loneliness of the freshman dorm and, tie-on-throat, made my way dutifully and apprehensively to a full card of fraternity rush dates. I have not, since that time, experienced a similar pseudo-social situation where a bunch of well-dressed, half-sloshed juveniles tried so hard to act sophisticated with a can of Schlitz in each hand. Each "frat" date was nearly identical, as was the insipid beer, the questions, and the feeling of being "rushed", i.e. hustled. But I succumbed, and "pledged" (promised to give inordinate quantities of my parent's money to the fraternity in exchange for access to booze, food, and lodging).

After having pledged, and made the first dues payment, hazing began. In the early 60's, somewhere in the US of A, a couple college freshman were killed during outlandish fraternity hazing rituals, and accordingly that *quid pro quo* process of "getting even for what was done to you as a freshman" was seemingly legislated into historical oblivion. The hue and cry for guilty parties was satiated by the spectacular and nationally followed court trials that supposedly brought sadistic hazing practices to a final and humanitarian halt. But in the 50's, hazing was akin to a primitive rites of passage ritual that winnowed out the geeks from the Greeks, which in reality and retrospect separated the intelligent drummers from the I'll-follow-you-anywhere dumbbells. As things turned out, I think hazing quickly identified those individuals who could think for themselves rather than submit to demeaning physical and emotional abuse as part of the herd/flock mentality: I submitted . . .

I obviously wasn't thinking for myself, as I, lemming-like, followed the leaderless pledges through denigrating day/night experiences of pain, embarrassment, induced sickness, trust erosion, and self-doubt. As I look back, waaay back, I can't think of any reason for this type of activity to continue, but it does: probably having something to do with that age and a desire to experience a rites of passage (more aptly, *wrongs of passage*), involvement which has been largely removed from our homogeneous, highly mobile, and pleasure-oriented society. The following detailed exercises in programmed sadism, are paradoxically masochistic because we asked for it, and it happened . . . 'cause I was there.

My son, Matt, recently pledged a fraternity at his college, and had the questionable opportunity of experiencing Hell Week bonding. After hearing some of his war stories, I was amazed at how little hazing has changed over the last 30 years. His tales (related enthusiastically with relish and scarcely hidden pride) although shocking, tasteless and probably embellished were, and probably are, common fare for the hapless fraternity initiate at any college in the country.

17

I have to admit that, although I think hazing of any kind is counter-productive, I enjoyed reminiscing from afar (30+ years) about the hard-to-believe stunts and fraternal mayhem that represent what I experienced as a frosh fraternal pledge. My current parental condemnation of hazing is largely a function of age, induced moralistic outrage (tuition money is being spent for what...?) and a more psychological and somewhat random anger that my personal rites of passage opportunities are becoming less available, and more socially acceptable.

I was nineteen at the beginning of my freshman year at college. I was fit, strong, and capable, if not somewhat naive and immature for my age. To my way of thinking at the time, I was not in college to pursue a career or seek higher learning; I was there to simply experience what the place had to offer and play some sports. Pledging a fraternity was part of that experience base, and, pragmatically, it provided me with a place to eat and sleep. At the time I didn't think of pledging or hazing as anything out of the ordinary, it was just part of the four-year college experience. I accepted all the degrading, ridiculous, demeaning pranks as readily as I accepted the college rules of dress, attending classes and not cheating. It didn't even enter my mind not to cooperate. Surviving Hell Week was challenging, representing simply another physical sports-like task to encounter and overcome. The only thing I would not allow (as mentioned below) was subjecting myself to repeated physical damage of my body.

Collegiate Hell Week is the culminating 5–10 day span that punctuates the absurdity of harassing a young person during that juncture in their academic career when they can least afford the time, energy or emotional commitment. The following "activities" either happened to me or I observed them being applied. There is no order, sequence, or logic to their presentation, which nicely parallels their use and abuse by the *brothers*—what a misnomer.

Paddling

Ash was definitely the wood of choice; resilient, attractive light grain, takes a high polish, exhibited low vibration on contact, and was extensively wallop-tested.

Of all the traditionally mindless and painful hazing activities, paddling was the most dreaded and, to my mind, the most demeaning of them all; so much so that, although I tolerated all the other sophomoric juvenile hazing stunts (not to my credit), I would not allow myself to be paddled repeatedly. I got away with this because (1) I was a big strong kid, and many of the potential paddlers weren't. (2) Even as a freshman I was a point-scoring member of the varsity swimming team, and they couldn't take a chance of injuring me. (3) I did not sign up for or express any interest in those arcane and highly secret honorary fraternities that took pride in breaking paddles and drawing blood.

However, I was hit often enough to know how much pain and damage some of the pledges were experiencing. The *brothers* would require that you "assume the position" for practically any infraction of the numerous and fatuous fraternity initiation rules. "The position" was standing in a bent forward posture, to best expose your gluteus as the target for the *descending ash.*

Most of the fire-ball paddlers were sophomores, getting even for what they had to endure the year before as part of their own hazing ritual. It was obvious though, that some junior and senior members derived puerile pleasure from delivering and/or watching the paddling. Many of the *brothers* did not paddle, in fact did not participate in a majority of the hazing activities, and I'm pleased to say I became one of the upperclass abstainers. I'm sorry to say, however, that I didn't suggest or make any moves to end hazing at my fraternity.

The following is a typically extreme wood-on-flesh scenario (corporal details included) that occurred at least once a day.

"OK, whale-s___, what's the founder's mother's name?" (Five seconds pass as the pledge's expression changes from aghast to resigned.) **"Wrong! Assume the position."** The pledge slowly bends over. **"What the hell is this?"** (The *brother* finds that the beleaguered pledge has padded his trousers in the gluteal area with cotton batting; there is considerable laughter from the spectating *brothers.*) **"You've had it now, s___ for brains. Drop trou'"**! (The pledge complains that he can't sit down for classes and...to no avail. The only padding left is the thin layer of Jockey cotton briefs that is already stained pink with fluid from the blisters of previous ash whacks.) The three sweeping blows (two additional for complaining) are delivered in cadence. The wood/flesh sound is devastating; sickening. No one laughs. The pink stain gets redder.

The You're-Pulling-My-Chain Scam

Early in the week we (the pledges), were instructed to tie an assigned flashy length of yarn to our testicles. The long end of the yarn was then passed up and under our shirts until the working end came out the front of the collar and hung obviously juxtaposed to the wearer's tie. All this was done to provide the *brothers* with a means of "checking discipline"; i.e., tugging on the end of the yarn.

Actually, the yarn was seldom tied to the genitals, but everyone (brothers and pledges) pretended that it was. A pledge squealed convincingly when the rare yank was given, but the physical harassment in this case was mostly imaginary.

de Sade's Delight

The following exercise in creative sadism must have evolved over a period of years: it's hard to imagine that one person could think of something this perverse by themselves.

The *brothers* presented us (the pledges) with a large block of ice to cool our fractured posteriors, but compassionate altruism was not the fraternal incentive. We were asked to strip down to our shoes (nakedness was a commonly used hazing tool) and take a closer look at the ice cake. The top of the block had been carefully sculptured to form an almost symmetrical concavity, about an inch and a half deep in the center and filled to overflowing with a crystal clear solution. It wasn't until later we discovered that the strong training room aroma emanated from the methyl salicylate that had been poured to the rim of the ice bowl. (Methyl salicylate is the stuff that makes Ben Gay smell like Ben Gay, and is also what puts the HOT in the word balm...like Atomic Balm. At that most center bowl-like location a moth ball had been delicately placed, which looked all the world like a white cherry in a surreal cocktail. I couldn't take my eyes off the perfectly still pool and the quintessentially placed white sphere; it was beautiful.

The challenge was ceremoniously explained by the pledge master, carefully and respectfully as if all knew that this was no ordinary hazing activity; this cheeky scam oozed of genius and tradition.

Each pledge was assigned their own moth ball, and was instructed to pick up that mentholated sphere from the center of the concavity with the cheeks of their gluteus maximus. Having pinched the moth ball securely in place (and having also deposited their individual scrotums and singular mucosal orifice amply into the innocuous appearing crystalline fire starter) the task remained to climb three flights of stairs and, without the use of hands, deposit the well-inserted moth ball into a Dixie cup situated on the top floor landing. If the ball missed the cup, or the cup fell over, the entire scenario had to be repeated—from the basement.

I don't think the insidiousness of this painful exercise can be appreciated by the reader, but imagine... When your anatomical parts made contact with the chilled chemical, there was no sensation other than cold. As you began to make your tight-cheeked way up stairs, the

20

exertion and skin friction opened the pores of your most tender parts allowing and causing the analgesic to do its torrid stuff.

After a couple trips up the stairs we were choking back tears. Then, in a planned paroxysm of compassion, that we should have recognized as a continuation of rehearsed sadism, the *brothers* kindly led us to the showers and suggested that we use **hot** water to wash off the vaseline-like analgesic. As the result of this single hazing stunt, there were individuals in that fraternity I did not trust for the remainder of my four years in college.

Have a Smoke!

I don't smoke now and I didn't smoke then . . . but we (ten naked freshman) smoked cigars together in a small (3' X 5') closet-like room used by the fraternity as a phone booth. We smoked and smoked and smoked (with the door closed, of course) until someone threw up . . . then smoked some more. This is obviously a fine activity to establish a sense of unselfconscious touch, trust, and a generous appreciation of abstract/textual fluid art.

More Technicolor Smile Material

At well-chosen meals (usually spaghetti), we were asked to toast the house mother (she was not there) with a glass of water from the various pitchers on the dining room table. Recognizing that we were such a jolly group, we were then asked to toast *brother* Browne, who had received a whopping C- on his economics quiz: bringing his semester average up to a D. Refilling our empty glasses with gusto, the brothers demanded that we toast the founding forefathers of the fraternity. (How could we refuse?)

Toasting everything and everyone continued until approximately 12 or so glasses of water had been tossed down, at which time they began coming back up in remarkably greater quantity and texture. We spent the remainder of the mealtime trying to rid the "dining" area of an unmistakable odor. More water was predictably released during this "clean up."

Subtle Pain

The *brothers* told us to take a break one evening and just lay face-down on the living room floor . . . and as a small additional task, they wanted to see if we could raise our arms over our heads and rest them on the floor also. With our biceps touching our ears, we began one of the most painful auto-induced experiences I can remember. There is nothing

21

more to the exercise than what I have explained... but, your arms had to remain over your head (ears on biceps). After an interminable time (perhaps an hour) we were commanded to get up immediately and jog in place. The amount of shoulder pain and immobility was impressive. It's something you might want to try some weekend when you don't have much to do.

Greaser

The pledges were divided into two teams and each team was provided with a five-gallon can of axle grease. As I remember, there was some rationale offered as to why we had to coat each other with the grease, but what resulted was an end in itself: 15 well-greased young men, whose every orifice was well packed and lubricated. Clothes were eventually discarded, but the greasy feel and automotive smell remained with us for days.

Eggs It Is !

Raw egg contents dropped from 20+ feet into the gaping maws of kneeling pledges provided great vicarious fun for the observing *brothers*. Even more fun, was to inject the eggs beforehand with asfiddida, an insidious chemical that rots eggs almost immediately.

It was not required that we swallow the eggs, which was beside the point anyway, as the fetid liquid contents had expanded during the drop to an area that nicely covered the entire face and head. Some yellowish contents sometimes made it into the oral (and nasal) cavity, and was inadvertently gagged down then up, but we were, by this time, well practiced in emptying our stomach contents.

When the week finally came to an end, all I remember is an evening of incongruous conviviality with a bunch of sadistic dolts that I had grown to actively dislike. That week caused more bad feelings and diminishing of trust than anything I had ever experienced. The talk about "brotherhood" and secrets shared (passwords and secret handshake—which I'll gladly share if you have a minute) was a joke, but apparently some of the people needed that sense of belonging, because they began to operate "in the bonds" as they used to say. The fraternity continued to be a place to eat and sleep for me, and I did make some good friends there as time went by, but I never trusted the fraternal organization after that pledging semester and culminating week of hell.

Thirty plus years later . . . it's just something to write about.

CHAPTER 4

O Positive Chum

"A truly wise man never plays
leapfrog with a unicorn."
"Banacek"

It's been over 30 years, and I'm still embarrassed about that *bloody* expedition. A naive attitude toward my own unrealistic sense of immortality didn't help much either. There's no getting around it, planning and attempting to implement that nutsy shark hunt was *really* skewed.

In 1962, I was working as an oil field roustabout for Richfield Oil Company in Long Beach, California; this was before the ARCO (Atlantic and Richfield Oil Companies) merger. I was also working part time in the evening as a medical technologist, a holdover from my military occupational specialty as a lab technician. "Join the army and learn a trade," as the recruiting advertisement used to read. As it turned out I didn't join, I was drafted, but I did learn a trade, in fact, I learned it better than most, operating as the self-professed "fastest needle in the West"—west of what, I'm not sure, but I was certainly impressed with my own prowess guiding a #18 needle into the brachial vein (and this was *before* disposal needles!).

My primary responsibility at the lab was as a phlebotomist, medical jargon for someone who draws blood: vampire, the sticker, red man, vein shooter—there were lots of inappropriate shibboleths, but the one I liked best was, "that guy." When the regular customers showed up for their prescribed blood sugar or CBC test, they would point to me and say, I want "that guy." I *was* good; fast and sweet. I didn't need one of those fire hose veins to make red contact, slipping that needle in (bevel up, that's the secret) so smooth and swift sometimes they didn't even know I'd been there. You know how it is when you do something right and everybody knows it? Well, I was *that guy*; maybe I should have stayed there.

The second part of my lab job was testing the collected blood and other secretions, leavings, and exudates that come from the human body. I didn't mind testing blood, liked it in fact, but I somehow missed the satisfaction of centrifuging urine, making sputum culture plates, or microscopically looking for fecal parasite eggs—kind of ruins your appetite, know what I mean? Say these words out loud to yourself, URINE, SPUTUM, FECES, . . . and how about PURULENT? How do you fill out a decent-sounding resume with words like that floating around?

A further adjunct to my lab responsibilities was making sure that the blood in the blood bank was kept up-to-date. Human blood, even when refrigerated, doesn't last long, having to be resupplied to the bank regularly, which is why the Red Cross is always looking for blood donors. The blood that is removed from the bank must be disposed of; remember this.

The oil field roustabout position wasn't much to speak of, just basic maintenance work around the pumps, but it was as dirty a job as I've ever had. Crude oil and oil residues got into and onto everything, including every orifice you owned. The smell of crude permeated your clothing and eventually, like garlic, became part of your body odor. The petroleum residues, even though scrubbed each evening, eventually became a permanent part of a worker's hand creases. It's easy to spot a full time oilfield worker, check out their hands and take a sniff.

Job benefits included the ostensible luxury of an employee shower on site, with special petroleum-cutting soaps available so that you didn't have to drive home reeking of crude. The company also made available a laundry stipend for cleaning oil-soaked clothing, and, although I'd like to say that the administration did this out of love for their fellow man, I can't, because they didn't. Employee health and bottom line concerns were at the root of this largesse. Without the special arrangements made for cleaning skin and clothing, many working hours would have been lost due to contact dermatitis and God knows what kind of internal ailments; not to mention the inevitable marital tiffs—talk about ring around the tub!

I was working at Richfield Oil Company because I had family responsibilities and my recently acquired B.S. degree in biology wasn't impressing any employers. Admittedly, part of the problem had to do with not wanting to take myself seriously . . . but, I'm still doing that. I was basically enjoying myself though; I had friends, some money, a physical lifestyle, *and I was young.*

My closest friend during this time was a fellow I had met in the army, John Herbert. John was taller and older than I, and there aren't many of those types around, so we hit it off well, besides, we both had an insatiable appetite for doing things the hard way. After being discharged (honorably), John and I decided to attend college together in Northern California because . . . we couldn't think of anything else to do.

After a semester of rainy weather (like every day), and average grades, college degree enthusiasm waned. We looked south toward warmer and drier weather, deciding that since we were both married, we needed responsible full time positions; so we planned to take the test to become Los Angeles beach lifeguards. Unfortunately, as it turned out, we lay in the sun too long before the swimming test (we hadn't seen the sun for a long time), and uh . . . well . . . failed the test. Knowing that our wives (still in Northern California) would be distressed, we immediately applied for work in the oil fields and were hired that day.

John and I spent quite a bit of our work break conversation time dreaming up different schemes to occupy our weekends in an exciting way (long distance off-shore canoe bashes, mountain climbing with minimum gear and even less experience, lobster and abalone forays, hunting deer with a .32 caliber pistol, etc.). I'm pretty sure we weren't pandering to any kind of personal adventure code, we were just two young, borderline irresponsible, married guys looking for something off-beat and physical to do on the weekends besides succumbing to household chores, or getting trapped by beer and TV.

In 1953, it was Howdy Doody Time, but in 1963, it was Jacques Cousteau time, and Jacques was my 9″ screen hero. I desperately wanted to do some of the things I watched Jacques do on TV, so that my weekends would be filled with dugongs, penguins, sea snakes, otters, orcas, and SHARKS. I was fascinated with sharks, drawn by the typical neophyte's ambivalence of fear and fascination, but the attraction wasn't entirely emotional or academic; *I wanted to harpoon one.* John was also definitely into Moby Dick role play, so we began planning and deciding what we needed for equipment to fulfill our seafaring fantasies.

Earlier, we had taken SCUBA lessons at a local dive shop. Barely able to afford the lessons, we couldn't afford much else, so we decided to try and fabricate a do-it-yourself wet suit; the water in Southern California is colder than you think. We figured that this low budget rubber suit would serve two purposes; extend our water time on future SCUBA outings, and serve as emergency cold water gear for this off shore shark hunt, just in the off chance we needed an exposure suit. Naive to the max!

On what I remember as a very hot day, I donned an old set of OD (olive drab) surplus wool long johns and tried to stand as still as possible while John painted me with green latex rubber paint. If there was any doubt in your mind about our personal commitment toward adventure, and our almost complete lack of technical and practical knowledge, this should be the clincher. The suit was a disaster; extremely uncomfortable, heavy, inflexible, embarrassing (it didn't work), and the green color was disgusting—I wish I had kept it for my personal museum of horrendous mistakes. John laughed a lot while he was painting me.

On a more positive note; during our earlier academic time spent in Northern California, we had purchased a 16' wood and canvas Old Town sponson model canoe. (Sponsons are bulbous flotation additions molded to each side of the canoe at the gunwale level. Sponsons provide some stability to a tippy canoe, but their use is somewhat off-set by the added weight and cumbersome addition to the canoe's width.) We only paid $60.00 for that fat canoe, an unbelievable bargain. Restored, that wood and canvas beauty would be worth well over $1,000 today. And we *did* restore it, venting some of our vicarious adventure frustrations by applying hands-on repair and loving restoration. As time went by, we even built from scratch, a lateen sail with an outrigger set up. This pseudo-polynesian rig was to be the harpoon platform for our shark hunting expedition. God, what were we thinking of?

With practically no slush funds available in our expedition kitty, and corporate sponsors hard to come by, everything either had to be scrounged, or built by hand. One of the fellows we worked with at Richfield was a drill-pipe welder, quite a bit older than John and I, but sympathetic to our adventure lust, and wanting to share vicariously in the hunt. He agreed to make the harpoon, and what a mighty spear it was. I wasn't much into photography at the time, so I have no photo of what that massive and terrifying amalgam of aluminum, steel, and brass looked like, but it was like holding adventure in your hands, a tactile reminder of all those things that mom told you not to do.

During work breaks, next to the welding shed, I frequently practiced my imagined throwing position, fantasizing the highlights of a successful hunt . . . *thrusting the wickedly barbed harpoon directly into the eye of a 30' white pointer, the ocean roiled red as the small outrigger struggled to remain upright amidst the pink foam and wild thrashing of the mortally wounded white shark.* Wow, straight out of Argosy mag . . . and I'm there!

But first, we had more to do; the canoe needed to be rigged. We found some large pieces of Styrofoam that had washed up on the beach, and after some rough shaping, jammed them as far fore and aft as we could, to act as flotation just in case... A couple truncated plastic Clorox bottles leashed with nylon cords to the thwarts would serve as efficient bailers in case we took on some water. Using some of that same cord, we lashed our diving knives to the same thwarts. The outrigger was solidly attached and the sail was ready to be rigged. What more could we possibly do, besides think of consequences?

A derrick foremen gave us an old hemp section of rescue line from one of the oil rigs. It was a bit ragged and oil soaked, but it seemed to be long enough, water beaded on its surface, and the price was right. This high quality length of rope would connect the one and only harpoon to the bow of the canoe; which was also a one and only, as were John and I. It's strange and frightening in retrospect as to what primo priorities are assigned to things in the flush of adventure.

The remainder of the preparations was all small stuff that we could put together at the last minute; knife, food, drinks, clothing, sunglasses. But there was one essential detail that had not been considered, and which slowed down the expedition a couple weeks (we could only consider doing this on weekends); what were we going to use for bait? What would Cousteau use? Well, that's obvious, he would throw over a couple goat carcasses, and maybe some pig guts, but our boat and budget didn't fit the abattoir scenario. We did consider asking for some meat scraps at the local butcher shop, but . . .

One evening at the lab, I had the perfect idea. Rather than throwing away the blood that was outdated, we could slice the pint bags at sea *and let human blood attract the sharks.* Everyone knew that sharks were attracted to human blood like magnets. Yahoo! We'd soon have sharks schooling around the canoe like mullets.

I recently performed a personal penance by writing the end of this story, but I'm sorry that I can't include it here, it's just too unbelievably stupid. Considering the innumerable mistakes and unconscionable decisions connected with this sea-going debacle, I'm just pleased to still be here.

Imagine instead that we were a couple miles off shore in that 16' sliver of a canoe, and were dripping O positive blood (and maybe some A negative) into the sea, onto ourselves, and into the canoe (. . . the bilge was running red!). Also try to imagine that large sub-sea creatures swam near the canoe, and that one of us (who used to throw the javelin in college) solidly harpooned one of these creatures, and further imagine the large gray creature diving straight down, causing the bow of the canoe, with the old rope attached, to pitch forward at a frightening angle, flipping the startled harpoonist and friend into the creature filled sea. Then the rope broke, and . . .

We made it back to shore sans harpoon, rope, blood, knives, and practically everything else that was in the canoe (except the Clorox bottles), with a poignant appreciation of what could have happen if the rope had not parted. But we were young and immortal, just like our children now, and we stumbled on to the next adventure somewhat chastened, but still full of the life that causes the next adventure to happen.

With the current stringent controls on blood collection and storage, I'm sure and comforted that used blood can no longer be so easily obtained or so cavalierly used.

> *"Tell me, old timer, where did you get your good judgement?"*
>
> **"Experience."**
>
> *"And how did you get your experience?"*
>
> **"Bad Judgement!"**

CHAPTER 5

Catalina Canoe

*"The fear more sick than the fear of death, more
dreaded than the fear of failure . . . fear of medocrity.
The excruciating fear of a life without passion."*

Mark Jenkins

A couple months after the California shark hunting debacle, John and I began training for a long distance canoe trip, from Long Beach to Catalina Island, a distance of some 23 open ocean miles. We put in a few practice trips up and down the shore line of about equal length, but never paddled more than three miles off shore. We planned not to use a companion boat because that would obviously reduce the adventure, but more to the point, we couldn't find anyone to follow us. We also did not think decking the canoe would be necessary, because we still had our two cut-off Clorox bottles to use as bailers.

We had postponed the trip a couple times because of bad weather, and because of a questionable forecast, it looked like we would have to postpone again, however my quest quotient was not to be denied, so on the evening of our next day departure I telephoned John and told him, weather or not, to be ready at 4:00 AM for an early start. He sheepishly answered that his wife was not at all happy about this particular trip (she was still a bit dismayed about the shark hunt) and was particularly disturbed because of our decision to shove off despite the predicted bad weather, and that to maintain a modicum of marital wa . . . he couldn't (shouldn't) go. Damn!

I couldn't believe it. John wasn't going, and our chance for canoeing immortality was being dashed upon the rocks of conservatism. It was only 20 some miles across the Catalina channel, a mere 5–6 hours of hard paddling, then we could either take the ferry back or perhaps even spend the night (I used to live and teach in Avalon) and paddle back the next day.

It's unbelievable how misguided confidence, youth, and a sense of predestination can result in such imaginative and unrealistic expectations. I suppose that's how impossible things get done, but it also results in a much higher proportion of improbable failures that you never hear about.

D-day dawned overcast and calm. Soon after sunup, I walked the short distance from my apartment to the beach, disgruntled and still convinced that we should have left two hours ago. There was NO wind, and the ocean was like a mill pond. Damn! We could be near halfway across by now.

Bare feet splayed in the sand, I stood peering despondently toward the darkened silhouette of an island that wasn't getting any closer. A freshet of wind snaked about my legs stirring the sand. Within ten minutes, that singular puff had become a steady fifteen knot breeze, and before another ten had slipped by, the breeze had become a constant series of hammer-like gusts. Coupled with the now driving rain, the ocean scene beyond the breakwater was six-foot seas and almost pure white caps.

I wouldn't have said it at the time, and don't know if I ever did, but, *thanks for saving our, lives Dotty.*

P.S.

While training for the trip we never made, John and I spent quite a bit of paddle time, switch stroking up and down the Southern California beaches. A favorite workout was the trip from Long Beach to Corona Del Mar, if you're familiar with that stretch of shore.

I used to paddle in the bow, as John had done a considerable amount of canoe tripping at summer camps, and was more comfortable J-stroking in the stern. I preferred the bow seat because I got to set the stroke tempo and from there enjoyed watching the bow wake. The bow was a power position that depended more on strength and endurance than skill and touch; I liked that.

One calm summer day, early in the morning, about two miles offshore, we had been paddling smoothly for an hour or so when I heard a **WOOSHING** sound, looked up and saw a huge mass of dark flesh rise above the calm ocean surface about 400 yards dead ahead. I half choked on my shout, "WHALE!" (I should have yelled, **SHE BLOWS!**, but I blew it.) I spun half around on my cane seat to face John, who, sat slack jawed with a dripping paddle held in mid-stroke, as if he were at parade rest with a rifle. I excitedly reacted, "let's get closer," swiveled back to my forward position and dug the paddle in for a few rapid-gain-momentum strokes.

After about six pulls on the paddle, I sensed the canoe wasn't responding to my power strokes, in fact we seemed to be drifting backwards! I tried a few more strokes with the same result. It even flashed through my mind that a whale might have breached beneath the canoe. I turned again toward John, puzzled and concerned, to see my powerful canoeing partner intently *back watering as fast as he could handle the paddle.*

33

CHAPTER 6

Frank

"Everything is a subject on which
there is not much to be said."

C.S. Lewis

In the early sixties, I worked for about a year as a medical technologist at a geriatrics clinic in Southern California. I had spent the two previous years as an army lab technician, and had transferred that training and experience to this current civilian job until I figured out what I *really* wanted to do.

While in the army, I spent considerable time and effort trying to convince the brass that I was certainly more valuable to the military establishment as an athlete than a "white coat." And I was partially successful, spending quite a bit of TDY (temporary duty) swimming and throwing things for various U.S. Army teams, but, as it turned out, most of my working time on post was spent in a windowless room, drawing and testing blood. Things could have been worse, I might have been assigned to permanent morgue duty, or designated to assist the OJT (on-the-job training) dental surgeons: "open wide, suction here, spit there"—terrible stuff.

I drew gallons and gallons of blood, and established myself as being just about the fastest needle in the west. If there was someone who, because of excessive adipose tissue or "collapsed veins," wanted an experienced blood-letter to work on them, I was the self-chosen *fast gun*. Drawing blood efficiently and painlessly is a matter of confidence and anatomical know-how. I was confident to a fault, and my needle was attracted to veins like a dowser's witch stick to water.

That confidence followed me to the civilian job, and my soon established reputation as a quick needle caused the other "techs" to defer tough cases (no visible veins) to me. Even so, I was surprised when Pat (a tech about my age, and also pretty good with a syringe) asked me to draw blood from Frank. Here's the story . . .

One morning at the lab, a very old and painfully thin gentleman sat down slooowly (by-the-numbers) next to my blood-letting chair; kind of a technical loveseat arrangement. His name was Frank and I found out later that he was 93. His initial movements toward the chair were controlled and labored, until the slow-moving levers of his old joints and bones passed their muscular control point and gravity took over, at which point his body mass collapsed toward the chosen target.

Frank's veins were extremely prominent, standing out in bas-relief against his painfully thin arms and hands. With a cursory look at the hemotology worksheet, and a brief hello (Howzit goin' Frank?), I readied my blood-letting tools and applied a rubber constrictor band just above the elbow. I wasn't exactly jaded to the job, but Frank was essentially just another vein, albeit an easy one.

With the needle angled and centered on his huge brachial vein, I casually applied well-practiced and deft pressure to the syringe body, but as quickly as you could say "ultra-sharp," the tip of the needle slipped to the side of the vein with a distinct grating sound, entering deeply into the flesh of his thin arm.

*I FLAT-OUT MISSED THE BIGGEST HEMO-TARGET THAT HAD EVER VISITED OUR LAB!**

My stoic patient didn't cry out or flinch in the least, but looking straight ahead, he leaned toward me and said in a hoarse whisper, *"Save me."* Not believing what I heard, and thinking that he needed help because of the pain I must have caused him, I answered in confusion, "What do you mean?" Same response, same whisper. *"Save me."* Drawing on all my humanistic training, geriatric experience, and the pathos of the moment, I formulated what I'm sure was the most inane response imaginable, "Save you from what?" Still leaning forward, he turned his head slowly toward me and offered a well-modulated two word answer that was not in the least tinged with humor, **"My wife!"**

Almost simultaneously, a loud, immediately obnoxious older woman with thinning blue/white hair stormed into the lab looking for her "lazy husband" (my thick-veined patient). Frank visibly cringed, and I realized that although his mind and body had deteriorated with age, he was absolutely serious about wanting to be saved. As he reluctantly got up to leave, amidst this harridan's complaints and vituperous comments about his slowness, Frank must have known that his only salvation lay beyond this life. (I did get the blood sample, but only by severely pinning down his heavily sclerocized vein, and applying an extraordinary amount of pressure to the needle.)

I learned a few weeks later that Frank had died soon after that blood test. The vile woman, who I'm sure made his last days uncomfortably long, was 74 years old, and had married him only six months prior to the lab visit. It didn't take a detective's intuition to figure out the intricacies of the legal but immoral insurance scenario that had been foisted on this defenseless old man. Unless that woman is now 105 years old, she's joined Frank, and I'll betcha he didn't save a place for her.

Frank was suffering from a number of ailments, but one of his conditions was extremely high blood pressure caused by almost solidly sclerotic veins. His vessels had become almost filled with sand-like deposits; very hard and noisy to penetrate with a needle.

The Plastic Pigeon

"You get what you get, when you go for it."
Barry Manilow

1972 was a good year for adventure. Having just the year before initiated an in-school program titled *Project Adventure*, it seemed only fitting that the staff attempt to accomplish high profile adventurous type things, so the curriculum door swung open to new ideas and schemes. Buying and building a hang glider . . . why not?

I had done some reading about hang gliding and was convinced that using the inherent excitement surrounding human flight, the regional high school students would become turned on to both the science of flying and the hands-on practicality of building their own flight mechanism. Amongst the students and most of the staff, no one believed that we could or would, build and fly a hang glider at the high school.

I couldn't get the experience and information that I needed from a book, so I began looking around for some other folks who were turned on to human glider flight. Soon thereafter, I located a hang gliding club in the Boston area that held monthly meetings at Newton High School. I attended three meetings, just enough to find out what I needed to know and see if I was on the right track. Surprisingly, the club was made up mostly of people who had never tried hang gliding, I suppose because, at the time, hang gliding in New England was considered such a new and esoteric sport.

On a sunny Saturday, I showed up at Newton High for a practice flight session sponsored by the club. Our take-off and landing area was the surprisingly large and multi-level grassed area in front of the school.

Our neophyte group of thrill-seekers numbered about 3 or 4. As I remember, that Saturday was a pleasantly cool day in the fall with practically no wind. The instructor was a young fellow who owned a couple gliders, and from what I had heard, competed nationally in hang gliding competitions. We were impressed by what he had accomplished in this new and exciting sport, and I think he was, too. He spent some time assuaging our obvious fears and explaining the dynamics of flight as it applied to these fragile-looking human "kites"; ground school, so to speak. I didn't pay much attention to the safety spiel because, honestly, the Newton slopes were not very intimidating;

high angle take-offs and soaring were definitely not part of the flight scene at Newton High.

I watched an older guy (older then me) hoist a glider, and take a run down the slopes. He did a lot of tippy-toe, alternating slope-sliding, before he reached the bottom, but recorded no air time. Watching someone who doesn't know what they are doing, try to fly an awkwardly carried combination of brightly-colored sail and aluminum tubes down and across a series of terraced grass slopes is just what you would imagine, flat-out funny. Then a younger and very serious woman tried some similar slope hopping with an equal lack of success. Both flailing attempts seemed out of control and counter to the grace and flow that I had imagined would be part of the experience.

It was my turn. I probably didn't look much better than the other two potential pilots, but I had learned something from their disjointed attempts, they didn't physically commit and give themselves up to the glider, trying rather to cognitively fly. I committed, running like the dickens downhill without flaring the wing (flaring acts as an air brake), and was rewarded with about 2–3 seconds of FLIGHT. It was just a brief bounce off the ground, but there was no doubt that I had flown. I was dutifully cheered by my clubmates, a scene very reminiscent of a Monty Python skit. I smiled in spite of myself, having approached my airborne baptism almost as seriously as my female predecessor. This uniqueness was exactly what I wanted the students to experience, but not necessarily the cheering part. I was doubly pleased, having experienced gliding *and* feeling justified that I had made the right decision to pursue this flight fantasy.

I tried a couple more "hops" down the hill, recognizing with some disappointment, that what I had initially experienced was about all the hill had to offer. I thanked the instructor, said so long to my boon flight companions, and mentally quit the club; they had provided me with all I needed to know and the Newton slopes were already too low and slow.

Using what I had learned via the club meetings, I shopped around carefully in order to buy the "glider makings" from the most reputable and available hang gliding supplier in the New England area, and considering that there was only one company selling kits, the yellow pages search was considerably simplified. Having spent at least five minutes finding the number for this arcane "kite" company, I called, convinced that I should buy what was needed immediately before all of New England discovered this burgeoning sport. However, after some in-depth discussion, I was convinced by some of the more conservative PA staff members (all of them, and none of whom accompanied me to Newton) that perhaps I should visit this flight factory first and get a consumer's feel for the owner, quality of the equipment, number of successful sales, customer satisfaction, and how many of the customers were still living.

Unfortunately, eighteen years has robbed my steel-trap memory of the company's name, but I remember the owner as a gruff, cigar-chomping fellow in his 40's, with a severe limp that hinted of a story I didn't want to hear. During our generally pleasant and mostly one-sided unintelligible conversation (this man wallowed in the jargon of flight and free-fall esoteria) he related his previous occupation as a parachute "test pilot," regaling me, midst clouds of stogie smoke, with high-flying tales of wind-sucking, nylon flapping adventure. I was intimidated yet taken in by his untempered bravado. He said all the things I didn't want to hear or imagine about kite failures and mangled riders, but the more he emphasized the possible implications the more I wanted the vehicle. He wouldn't " . . . *sell these kits to just anyone*"," but for some reason, that I suspect had to do with *dinero*, he sold me everything I needed to put in some serious air time.

I returned to the Regional High School with my treasures and a tingling sense of having been hustled by a pro. But for all I've said in jest, the purchased materials and gear were obviously top-notch; it was now up to me to assemble the myriad pieces in a conscientious and FAA-approved way.

Project Adventure in 1972 was still located in a single converted classroom at the Regional High School in Hamilton, Massachusetts. The room was barely large enough for the 5 staff, so converting part of it into a hang glider production area was not well received by four of the five. Fortunately, and as it turned out serendipitously, our first floor room (all the rooms at the Regional are first floor) looked out onto a large courtyard that was mostly empty. What a great high profile place to assemble a hang glider.

Those of you presently employed at a school are bound to be thinking, "How did he get permission to buy a hang glider kit, assemble it on school property, use the students as hands-on workers, and eventually plan to use those same students as pilots?" The answer is, we were *Project Adventure*, and for at least the first couple years of operation, the solid support for our beyond-belief curriculum was there for the risking. We even taught mouth to mouth resuscitation without Annie; i.e., using mouth-to-mouth contact . . . but that's another story.

With no background in engineering, metal work, or any type of fabrication that resembled what I was attempting, I threw myself at the task and following Tom Watson's advice (at one time, IBM's president), "Success is full of failures, lots of them." failed a lot. But true to Tom's advice, each fractional failure taught me something.

There's an important shading of interpretation concerning the function of failure that I have to mention. Failing at something (not achieving what you are attempting to do) is useful only if the failee cares about the task, and is able to learn something from his/her mistakes. It's easy to quote someone who has been successful, particularly if their quote is tidy and rings true, but implementation is often quite another story. To a motivated person, Watson's "failures" are a goad to further attempts. To a chronically inept player, one more failure is another slow-motion frame in their ". . . agony of defeat".

Interest abounded in the court-yard as I rebounded from a series of learning mistakes. The students and I were learning an exotic vocabulary, a number of esoteric skills, and developing a high tolerance for answering the same inane questions over and over. "Are you really going to . . .?" "What's this thing for?" and "Can you fly it out of here?"

The minimal fuselage was done and hinted of future flight fantasies. With the frame completed, the issue of wing flight surface caused much discussion and uninformed debate. The deep pocket advocates wanted to purchase a ready-made sail (wing material) of brightly colored and durable Dacron. The cost of the sail alone doubled the price of the kit, but what a temptation. The other alternatives were to shape, cut, and sew a polyester sail ourselves (a daunting task, even for those dedicated to multiple failures along the way) or try an inexpensive procedure that I had read about in some tabloid adventure mag; to make the sail from sheets of nylon reinforced poly tarp material; i.e., plastic, and duct tape it to the frame.

Because PA's then director was a frugal fellow, we operated in the field with fairly low tech material. Winter camping trips with the students during that time used 1/4" ensolite pads, World War 11 wooden cross country skis, and 6 mil poly tarp plastic for the tents. No problem really, in fact I think the students gained a greater appreciation for good gear after having experienced what the GI's and 1950's Sierra Club hikers used.

However, since we had lots of poly tarp material around, I cut a section to fit our 18 foot long wing span and found out why so many people bought a ready-made sail. The "poly" just wasn't strong enough to work with and engender that feeling of trust that allowed adventuring beyond the expected. Eventually, a call to the distributor of the poly material indicated that there was a product similar to the 6 mil sheets, but strengthened with strips of nylon imbedded in the plastic; obviously just right for our intended use. And it was . . . well . . . not just right, but close enough.

43

The hang glider was finished. We even had a home stitched hang harness to suspend us beneath our fantasy machine. (Read **Parachute Perambulations**—same harness.) Remembering how little actual air time we eventually recorded in that harness, I'm impressed at the amount of fantasy fulfillment that was achieved before the vehicle was ready for use. The hours of imagined flight far outweighed the actual seconds (maybe minutes) that were actually logged, giving further weight to the opinion that programmatically, preparation is more educationally valuable than the act of implementation.

I tried a bit of "safe" flying off the football field (the field and surrounding areas were dead flat) by hoisting the glider and running into a stiff breeze. My image was not enhanced by these attempts, as the flukey cross-field winds caused me to run tippy toe, and more than once completely up-ended the kite, without so much as recording a second of air time (unless you count the micro-seconds I spent being flipped over and thrashed by my new wind toy). There had to be a safer and more aesthetic location.

In my eager state of ultimate naivete, I considered any location that put my head higher than my feet as a potential launch site. For those of you familiar with the Hamilton area, I even knocked on the door of the old Ayer's estate home (the one that has since burned down) to see if it would be okay to use their front lawn hill as a flight site. I was unconsciously presumptuous to the extreme. (A butler answered the door and in a haughty voice and demeanor that was straight from a grade B Hollywood scene, said "Mrs. Ayers is not at home. Would you please leave your request in writing.") As it turned out, I didn't use that site, or write the note, but I did break my finger there three years later on the same hill trying to "get some air" over a snow-covered log on cross country skis.

I also tried to get some air on the Hamilton ski slope with the Pigeon, but didn't break anything except a sweat on that day. It was in July and the temperature must have been 90+, without a breath of wind. I galloped down and staggered up that hill too many times. The Plastic Pigeon and I were spending a lot of time together, and all of it on the ground.

Remembering an article I had read about hang gliding, the author had waxed eloquent about how easy it was to launch from a sand dune. I think the specific location mentioned were the massive dunes on Cape Cod. In the local town of Ipswich, Crane's Beach had a few sand hills that weren't near the height of the Cape Cod dunes, but I wasn't looking for world records, just a simple airborne return on a lot of effort and image.

It worked. The take-off dune measured no more than 25′ top to bottom, but with a decent head wind the Pigeon bloused its plastic wing and tugged me free of the sand for a couple hundred feet. Wow! This was exciting! The fellow I was with and I traded rides for the next hour or so, until one of us snapped a wing tip on landing. I had no idea at the time that this type of damage was to be repeated over and over during student landings. But on that day we trudged home fulfilled with warm weather memories of fractional flight.

I never did get a great number of students to try flying off those dunes, certainly not enough to justify the expense and time expended, but I talked a few "pigeons" into visiting the beach, watching a couple glides and giving it a try if they wanted to; the ole adventure suck-'em-in routine.

Situated on top of the highest dune, I'd stand behind the glider with my hand on the keel, tell the student to run hard off the end of the dune, then I'd run with them, shoving forcefully on the frame as they launched. The combination of the head wind, their impetus and my push was usually enough to get at least 100 feet of glide.

On one occasion, a student kicked off the dune so hard that his foot got caught in the trapeze control bar cables so that his piloting position was essentially upside down, resulting in initial cranial contact with the sand below. I congratulated myself on picking such a soft landing area and tough pilot, convinced that nothing worse could happen.

During all those dune jumping flights, the only things that got broken were multiple wing tips, and they became harder and more tedious to fix. The entire kite was taking quite a beating from a gang of novices, and I was quickly wearying of the repair responsibility, so when the officials at Crane's Beach said that we were attracting too much attention and were jeopardizing our personal safety, I smilingly agreed and put the hang glider away for the season, secretly knowing that it was being retired for good—for my good.

As I write this in December of 1990, 18 years after what became known as Pigeon Follies, I could, at this moment, go to where the trapeze control bar is currently stored. The poly tarp wing material was cut up and recycled for sleeping bag ground covers. The high-grade aluminum tubing that made up the wing struts was used for a variety of domestic and work-related tasks over the years, and the various pieces of connecting hardware were used for other projects or discarded.

The thing I like to remember about Project Adventure during the early 70's was that we WERE adventurous. It was a heady time of pre-granted permission for nutty ideas that we were crazy enough to try and implement. It was a wonderfully creative and exciting experience;

I'm happy to have been there. And I'm still happy to be there, which is here . . . right now.

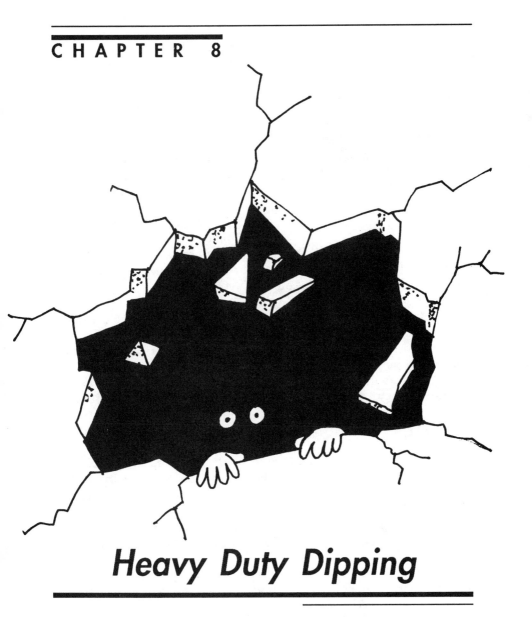

CHAPTER 8

Heavy Duty Dipping

*"If I'm going to be challenged, I'd
rather it be while I'm comfortable."*

KER

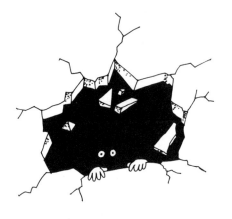

I've had that picture on the wall of my office for years, I guess to remind me that at one time I was a lot more tolerant of cold weather pursuits than I am now. The photograph shows Bob Lentz and I frozen by a flash, also literally frozen in our jockeys on top of a half submerged, snow-covered row boat. In the photo, the snow on the boat is also coldly displayed in stark contrast and greater abundance on the shore line behind us. Our mandatory "say cheese" frozen smiles are just that. Not seen on film, but also indicative of our near hypothermic state, is the contracted *in vitro* position of our frightened testicles.

This photo was taken during one of Project Adventure's early ski touring winter trips. Seasonally we would advertise some cold weather camping *fun* in New Hampshire and would invariably end up with 25–30 high school students who wanted an answer to the ultimate winter camping conundrum, "What's the reasin' for freezin'?" We didn't provide the answer, at least one they wanted to hear, but we continued the trips because we were an adventure based program, we had the right gear, we had a student population that volunteered for the experience, and New Hampshire had the right stuff; i.e., cold and snow.

During those winter treks, we regularly bussed to our jumping-off spot, then slogged and slid (mostly slogged) on ancient surplus 10th Army Mountain Division wooden skis to a small semi-wilderness pond area for a day of cold acclimatization and ski touring practice. I am not a fan of cold weather sports by any comparison, but have to admit that even our ineffectual slip-sliding along the forest trails was a unique experience, and occasionally fun.

The remainder of the trip consisted of travelling from one camp spot to another, living out the kind of gritty hardships that parents want their children to experience, and are convinced that *they* experienced daily as part of their own childhood. "Why, when I was a kid, we didn't have buses pick us up for school. I walked three miles to and from classes no matter what the weather, and didn't miss a day; except when I had to help Ma and Pa milk the cows, bale hay, pluck chickens, plow the fields . . ."

Sitting in the bus on the way home, unzipped with Patagonia labels well displayed, I'm sure the majority of the participants were proud of what they had physically accomplished and would probably say they had enjoyed themselves; definitely one of those million dollar experiences that you wouldn't attempt again for a nickel. But this is all preparatory pedagogic palaver for the main event of this frigid discourse, *heavy duty dipping.*

At the end of the third day we would invariably be camped next to and sometimes on a small lake. Preparations for the evening activity would begin early in the late afternoon, as skiers substituted insulated boots for skis and begin hauling dead wood to the center of the pond. It's amazing how much wood can be collected by a group of thirty people that have nothing else to do but keep themselves warm.

By the time darkness made further wood collecting impractical, the established pile was at least 15 feet high. The potential for warmth and light was anticipated with great interest, in addition to the elemental hunter/trapper's atavistic desire for spiritual fire. A fire to stand near, a fire to stare into, a fire to share the elemental bonding of our large brained species, and a fire for the ceremonial DIP. (Interestingly, no matter how hot or high the evening flames roared, the base of the fire never melted more than 1/2" into the lake ice; a teachable moment.)

In anticipation of this ritualistic cold water immersion, we used ice axes to chop out a bathtub-sized pit in the three-foot thick ice. (All our frosty campers by this time knew that to get water from the lake for drinking and food preparation, a narrow hole had to be chopped through the thick mid-winter ice. When the final breakthrough was made, the cold pond water burbled and surged through the cut hole, rapidly filling the excavated area in the ice until the water, seeking its own level, stopped just short of spilling out on the the surface ice.) When the tub was finished (smoothed, rounded, and measuring perhaps 5' long by 3' wide by 30" deep), the pick end of the ice axe was used to continue a small vertical hole the last 6" or so to reach water. What a joy, after so much work, to see water gush into the hole, rapidly filling your sweat-earned dip basin.

The students were amazed by the amount of work required to dig an ice tub of this size and fascinated by the hands-on physics lesson (water seeking its own level) being manifested right in front of them. They wanted to know, of course, what the tub was for, since we had already established a couple other holes for camp water use. We told them that the shimmering, slush covered pool was to keep fresh any fish we happened to catch and for ceremonial dipping. They astutely commented that we had not brought any fishing gear and that no one was fishing. Right! So, I guess we had better explain the latter function.

Later that evening, for those who chose to join the *frozen buns club,* a fifteen minute run around the lake was scheduled. This preparatory jog was made in full winter dress to insure the formation of a thin layer of warm moisture on the skin, indicating that it was time to rid ourselves of excess clothing and slip our overheated bods into the "cooling pool." The slush dipper could luxuriate in this pool as long as they liked (usually not much longer than 0.8 seconds) then join the other dippers in a rapid stroll to the now blazing pond center fire. The dip was not deemed official unless the participant's entire person was immersed. (Lest you think that we were dipping *al fresco—au naturel,* each student was required to wear a set of modest opaque dipping attire, which varied considerably person to person.)

Standing by the fire after the dip was a rare treat, and provided useful biological proof that a warmed human body does not crack when immersed in ice water, then exposed to open heat. The bonfire flames and coals threw out an almost intolerable blast of heat, which nicely toasted our frosted buns, but also allowed the ventral part of our warming package (the side facing the frozen woods) to feel the penetrating chill of the night. It was an odd and frightening sensation to have the dorsal half of your body toasty warm and the ventral half distinctly cold, depending upon your fireside orientation, of course.

This ice water dip became an annual winter trip happening; a scheduled unrealistic expectation, so to speak. There was no pressure put on any of the students to participate, but we would regularly get about half to make the plunge by creating a shared challenge situation, and by volunteering to make the dip first ourselves; i.e., leading the way. The more prudent campers took great delight in watching and making appropriately crude and incisive remarks. It was all great fun, and everyone seemed to enjoy the evening shenanigans, until the year Louise continued her dip *beneath the ice.*

Lou was a Project Adventure regular, having attended many other PA functions, including the year's previous winter trip. During that first winter experience, she had made the decision not to take an ice dip, but like everyone else seemed to join in the fun and camaraderie of the situation. She said nothing about the dip scenario at the time or even later as we debriefed the trip with the student participants. I thought it somewhat odd at the time that she didn't go for the dip, because of her *Go For It* attitude, but she never mentioned anything about that evening and neither did I. As the seasons unfolded, Lou continued to join us on PA trips and functions, still operating in her open, and infectiously enthusiastic manner. I was not surprised when she signed up for the next year's winter trip.

The temperatures during that February had been comparatively mild, so the ice depth was easily 10″ less than in years past. When we industriously dug out our ice tub for the ceremonial dip, half the tub's bottom was inadvertently chopped away as the result of the unexpectedly thinner ice. Looking down into the tub was frightening because of what the black unknown half represented, but we were confident that the students would be okay simply sitting in the tub and getting right out, as it would have taken a conscious effort to slide a body vertically through the dark half. Considering the average dip time at less than half a second, the chances of wiggling into the hole seem miniscule, well within our *calculated abandon* modus operandi.

That evening, when it was time for the dip, the multi-year tradition once again played itself out, and I was not surprised that Lou had decided to join us. Half a dozen kids made their frozen plunge, as we carefully instructed each dipper to stay in the ice bottom half of the tub. It was so dark by that time of the evening that the light and dark halves of the tub were covered with uniformly black water. Lou's turn came and she entered the tub with abundant confidence, and to everyone's surprise, sat back in the tub with her elbows resting on the pond ice surface as if she were enjoying a warm bath at home. She remained in that position for at least a full five seconds, a remarkable feat that I'm sure those of you who have been so intemperate as to jump into ice water will confirm. She looked up at me directly, smiled, then wiggled herself into a vertical position and without hesitation sank beneath the surface of the pitch black water. I can still picture her wide-open hands jutting from the icy water, then disappearing.

She remained under water for perhaps 2–3 seconds, then burst to the surface laughing, sputtering, and flopped immediately onto the surface of the pond ice. Lou was on her feet and sprinting toward the fire before any of the shocked observers could react. I had said nothing from the beginning of her dip to her exit run for the fire.

From the time of her initial entry into the tub until her explosive reappearance, no more than ten seconds had gone by, but I would have sworn it was closer to five minutes. Lou was an excellent student and a superior athlete and had been very disappointed the year before in her personal decision not to join the other ice dippers, so disappointed in fact that this year she had challenged herself to sit for five seconds in the icy slush; the trip beneath the ice was a spontaneous embellishment. She later admitted that her disappearing trick was a personal penance for having "chickened out" the year before.

51

During her short immersion beneath the black water, I found out something about myself that I didn't particularly like; I would not have gone beneath the ice after her. I was already on my way down to the hole in an attempt to reach under the ice, but I know now, as surely as I knew when she slipped under, that I would not have followed.

Talking with her later, she was very apologetic about the stunt and admitted that she had not thought about what our reactions and emotions would be as she disappeared beneath the water. Lou, in a mitigating gesture, admitted that she had never lost contact with the ice; her hands remaining hooked over the chopped ice hole, but considering the darkness of the night, to us she was essentially gone.

Personal growth often comes from achieving beyond what the individual thinks can be accomplished: Lou had achieved her goal. I'm not sure I benefited from the experience, but I found out something I wouldn't do, even when the stakes were the highest.

CHAPTER 9

Orange Parachuting

"It's not that I'm afraid to die, I just don't want to be there when it happens."
Woody Allen

always knew that I would make a parachute jump.

In 1968, I was a full-time employee at the *North Carolina Outward Bound School.* The school site is just on the edge of the Linville Gorge Wilderness area and about a fifteen mile drive over some terrible roads to the town of Morganton. Working as an instructor at *Outward Bound* was initially exciting but somewhat predictable during the winter months. I've never had a high tolerance for repetition, so during that bleak February I was casting about for something adventurous to do.

One of the other instructors, Dave Mashburn, had been a U.S. Army Ranger while in the service. During shooting-the-bull sessions we found out that becoming a Ranger involved various uncomfortable military training situations, one of which was airborne school; i.e., time spent learning how to jump out of airplanes. He regaled us with detailed "war stories" of what it was like to take a jump. I was fascinated with the procedure, the vehicle and the emotions surrounding what I perceived as an ultimate adventure; my questions were endless. Some of the other instructors had also parachuted at some point in their adventure/military careers. I had not.

Dave eventually gave in to my enthusiasm and said he would find out what was involved to plan a local jump. I still don't know why I felt so dependent upon Dave to make a simple yellow pages call, but it probably had to do with image, experience, and aura. As time passed (months), we finally arranged a date, and because of the same scheduling reasons that prevented us from spontaneously hopping in the car and driving to the jump site, we never pulled it off.

The only piece of memorabilia that I have from that time is the wallet-sized card (which cost ten dollars I couldn't afford) that indicated I was insured for landing on cars, cows and various other items of intrinsic value that my *controlled* descent might damage. There was nothing in the detailed disclaimer that said anything about insuring portions of my anatomy, but then what do you expect for ten bucks? So plummeting from a plane was shelved for a few years, while I got married, changed jobs, moved, had some children, and started getting bored again.

Project Adventure had been extant as an organization for about 6 years when the yearning to "fly down" returned. I had chanced on a small advertising pamphlet from the Orange Jump Center (near the town of Athol in Western Mass.) that detailed prices and procedure for a first jump scenario. Not wanting to keep all the fun and fear to myself, I passed around the flight invitation to other Project Adventure staff members in hopes that just a bit more convincing would tip my vacillating prelude to participation toward the DO IT end of the scale. Bob Lentz, then director and about my age, agreed to head out that way with me to "watch a few jumps," and . . . bring your checkbook just in case.

We arrived at the jump center on a beautiful late summer day. We looked at the printed materials, admired the impressive framed photos, perused the facility, smiled at each other (jointly recognizing why we had really made the drive) and decided, what the heck . . . We paid the fee ($125.00) and started our first jump lessons almost immediately.

The jump instructor was young, knowledgeable, well spoken, and confident. My only complaint was his penchant for disaster jokes. ". . . if everything goes wrong, you have 17 seconds from the jump altitude of 1,500 ft. to kiss your ass goodbye." We laughed. It wasn't funny.

After the initial talk (that was supposed to relax us), a vintage movie on sky diving that featured the Orange Jump Center was shown, and it became quickly obvious that it had been presented and seen many times previous to our tight cheeked sitting. Our confident instructor flipped the ON switch and quickly left the room. On cue, he returned seconds before the credits ended. Nice movie. Good timing.

From there, imbued with the cinematic safety, joy, and Zen of parachute jumping, we (the class numbered eight potential jumpers) headed for the outfitting room where we received the specialized gear necessary to jump and more pertinently at this juncture, to practice landing. I was definitely more concerned about how and where I would land than worrying about jumping. I figured that the odds were overwhelmingly in my favor that I would fall in the right direction, and that there was also a statistically excellent chance that one of the two chutes would open, but eventual contact with the ground (perhaps concrete, trees, electric cables, etc.) was still a somewhat nebulous although certain occurrence. I had heard that a parachute landing was like stepping off a three-foot high table; I didn't believe that.

During high school and college I had performed well at various sports, and had developed that certain cocky confidence that defines an individual who has achieved a high level of physical competence, often recognized in younger people as egotistical brashness. As such, we have found during PA workshops it is often the most physically adept (and not necessarily young participants) that have the most difficulty commiting themselves to a new activity, as fear of looking bad in a new situation becomes the barrier to participation.

I surprised myself by becoming anxious about how I would perform during the practice fall-and-roll training, about how I would *look*. Jumping from a couple thousand feet didn't seem very daunting, but stepping off a three foot platform and performing a simple roll gave me the anxiety sweats.

As part of a group of eight novices, I jumped, arched and rolled like the rest, until the instructor was sufficiently convinced that we wouldn't just fall out of the plane like a lump, or hit the ground with the same lumpish look. We learned a few things that seemed aimed at the sport of sky diving, but most of the training emphasis related to what could go wrong and what had to be done quickly to insure our continued enjoyment of the day. Considering that there were only 17 seconds to play with, from the jump altitude of 1,500 feet, I was grateful that they emphasized the intricacies of the second parachute, in fact I was wondering if there was precedent for a third chute . . . but I was afraid to ask.

We jumped from platforms of various height into the sand, all the while shouting "ARCH THOUSAND, TWO THOUSAND, THREE THOUSAND . . ." as a reminder to maintain a spread-eagle arched body position as you exited the plane. Without that spread, there was a good chance that, because of wind pressure, your lack of bilateral symmetry (predictable fetal position) would cause your bod to tumble severely, reducing the chance of a functional chute deployment. I was immediately into arching. I arched like my life depended on it . . . hmmm. I was definitely the best archer of the day.

Then, after a brief break for lunch that no one ate, it was time to suit up. This segment reminded me of being outfitted for military basic training, although the flight equipment fitted better, and the comparison between our jump instructor and the army training sergeant was no comparison at all. After tugging, fitting, and scrunching the parachute straps into what can best be described as very secure, we were told that there was to be no jump today because of deteriorating weather conditions. I had been so engrossed in the training and fitting I had paid no attention to the now noticeable scudding of the darkening clouds overhead. DAMN, no jump. All this and no jump. I was a bit relieved, but mostly disappointed.

There was nothing else to do, so Bob and I collected our "rain (wind) check" and headed home, talking on the way about what we thought of the training, our feelings, the instructors, and comparing the experience to the programmed adventure that we presented as part of the Project Adventure curriculum. And, of course, reinforcing one another's desire to get back out to Orange as soon as possible (male bonding at its best).

Quite a bit of time went by before I returned to Orange for that rain check jump. There was no reason for the delay, just some schedule conflicts and a bit of adventure ennui. Bob couldn't make the trip, so I talked a former Hamilton-Wenham PA student into accompanying me. He had not been through the initial ground training and enough time had gone by since my initial visit that I felt a few jumps into the sand would be useful, so we both sat through the movie, the inspirational talks, the black humor jokes, etc. Actually it was a confidence booster to repeat the training, and uniquely exciting to be in the student role again.

After lunch, for some reason, we had a change of instructor, but the young fellow that took up with our group seemed equally as knowledgeable and had a sense of humor that did not depend upon macabre jokes for a laugh. He (Sam—not his real name) made sure that we were fitted properly, tolerantly answered whatever inane nervous questions that we fabricated in rapid-fire fashion, and generally, by his calm manner, made us feel that our decision to give up a day in order to jump out of a functional airplane was at least semi-rational.

Completely fitted out and looking like a culinary class in our white jump suits, we filed into the two-prop plane that was to take us up to jump altitude. I was told that since I was the largest, it would be best if I jumped first. I still don't understand what my size had to do with jumping first, but I was keen, so I smilingly agreed, and took a seat right next to the exit door; I mean exit opening, there was no door. Looking around I had to smile at the incongruous sight of eight disparate citizens dressed in white (helmets too), queueing up and waiting patiently with forced smiles for our turn to have the shit scared out of us.

We arrived at jump altitude too quickly. Sam was sitting next to me and had been keeping up a constant patter of loud (the wind sound was practically overwhelming) conversation. I'm sure this was his way to assuage our very obvious concerns, and it worked—kind of. Looking over my shoulder and out the door and down, I had a sudden revelation: I wasn't frightened at all of the jump, I was afraid of dying. I knew I would jump when the time came (and the time was coming very soon), but I have to admit to poignant feelings of mortality, and wondering where I would be 15 minutes from then, hoping fervently that I would *be* somewhere. Sam stood up and looked nonchalantly out the door, and threw out a wind direction indicator. This comet ball-like device was used to see which direction the jumpers would float after the parachute opened. Apparently satisfied that my float potential was optimum, Sam mouthed something in my direction indicating by hand signal that I should join him at the DOOR (the hole in the fuselage). This was IT, *the real thing*—my heart rate was well above 60 bpm.

This was a static line jump, which means that I had a hefty section of nylon strap connecting me (my chute) to the plane. When I jumped, the strap would automatically pull out a small drogue chute that would then deploy the 32′ diameter main chute, and I would begin my gentle descent to the large circular sand DZ (drop zone) 1,500 feet below. If I just threw myself out the door, there was an excellent chance that I would begin tumbling and an equally excellent chance that my flailing arms and legs would become tangled in the chute lines. Thus the reason that Sam was pointing to a small metal step outside the door, on the wing. The step was actually a duplicate of what I had stood on a couple hours ago for practice, but I noticed a couple differences: I was now looking straight down from well over 1,000 feet, and a 100+ mph wind was trying to make me role play a two-string puppet. The noise of the wind and engine made verbal communication impossible.

After two tries I got my left foot on the wing step, letting my right leg "flap" in the wind. My hands were firmly (I mean FIRMLY) grasping the wing struts directly in front of my face; I was literally out of the plane. It was a moment to remember, but I didn't. I think at times of sensory overload the brain kicks out of gear, allowing you basic functions only (genetic responses to stimuli, urinating, etc.), but no sensory recording capability. In the midst of this cacophony of sound and wash of adrenaline I felt a tap, no, it was more like a hard slap on my shoulder. That was my signal to jump, and with a yell that I'm sure was more screech, I was arching off into a fast-forward gray area of which I have no memory. The next thing I do remember was silence and a full canopy overhead. I immediately looked for the plane and was amazed that it seem so far away and so far above me. The quiet was awesome, as was the expanded view twixt my toes.

An out-of-body voice said, "Nice jump, Karl" and then, "Now let's try a couple turns." I had forgotten about the radio receiver stashed at my sternum, but my friendly ground crew didn't let me forget for long. Before I could begin enjoying the descent, that smiley voice was leading me around the sky. So I pulled the toggles left and tugged the toggles right, and made my requisite turns as the disembodied voice kept telling me what a grand job I was doing (his congratulatory comments were earthier than that). My next look down was a shocker—everything was big and getting bigger faster. I was not floating at all, but experiencing a controlled plummet. Remembering not to look down as I neared the sand to avoid what they called "ground rush" I looked at the horizon and tried to remem . . . **WHAM! Down!** That was NOT like stepping off a three foot table. Damn . . . that about knocked the wind out of me. But I'm down, and lookin' good; not so bad really.

One of the support crew came over, perfunctorily congratulated me, then helped remove the straps and chute. He took the gear over to a van, and I stood there in the sand feeling pretty good about myself, but wondering what I should be doing. I started over to the van also, but thought, "Why not stay here and watch some of the other students make their landings?" Why not indeed, seems like that should be covered by the fee. So I watched with great interest as the other students jumped, descended, and landed with varying degrees of luck: I don't think we were at a level where you could associate anything we did with skill. After the last student jumped, I noticed the plane circling to gain altitude and that was the last thought I gave to it. About that time I began, somewhat euphorically, wandering toward the van where some of the other jumpers had collected.

I heard Sam before I saw him. My attention was drawn back to the sky by the sound of wildly flapping fabric, then almost immediately an emotional plea over the loudspeaker, "Open, Open... **OPEN!** My first reaction to the falling body was, "What a lousy joke" referring to what I thought was a dummy that had been thrown from the plane. It was no dummy, it was Sam and his chute had not opened, or had partially opened and wrapped around his body causing the loud popping/cracking wind sounds I had first heard. I was riveted by what I now knew, but didn't want to believe, was a rapidly unfolding tragedy.

When I first looked up, I could see Sam trying to free his chute, and there still seemed to be time for him to make an adjustment or release his reserve chute (I didn't realize at the time that he had already cut away his fouled main chute), As he fell further and his silhouetted body flashed across the horizon, I was astounded at the plummeting speed of his final seconds. He was a couple hundred feet above the ground, then he was part of the ground. The impact caused his rag-like body to rebound a few feet above the sand and then collapse into a heap that was barely visible from where I stood, about 200 feet away. Sam was dead. He had to be dead. No one could withstand an impact like that.

No one moved. The couple standing near me were newlyweds and had apparently decided to do something exciting on their honeymoon. The newly-married bride fainted. Still, no one moved toward Sam's body. I took a couple steps in that direction, not really wanting to but compelled by a feeling that someone had to do something. An emotionally terse voice over the loudspeaker told me to stay where I was. Still no one moved. I shouted, *"Isn't anyone going to help him?"*, instinctively knowing that no one could. One of the white-clad ground crew jogged to where Sam had impacted and leaned down. After a few seconds he looked up and said there was no pulse.

After a week or so I wrote a letter to the Jump Center, asking what had gone wrong. Their reply was polite, concise, and understanding. Sam (22 years old and a veteran of 250 previous jumps) had incorrectly adapted his reserve chute in some way that prevented complete deployment of the canopy lines. The mistake was obviously a fatal one.

I returned alone to Orange about eight months later, determined to "get back on the horse." I repeated the AM training, and jumped that afternoon out of a small two seater plane. I had no overriding fears about death except those images that hover just beyond rational thought. The exit from the plane was easier and more memorable—the gray time was minimal. The landing was even easier; more like the reported "three foot step off a table."

I looked around the circular sand DZ area. I tried not to look toward where Sam had impacted, but I did. It was something that happened a long time ago.

The above scenario occurred in 1977. I have not jumped since.

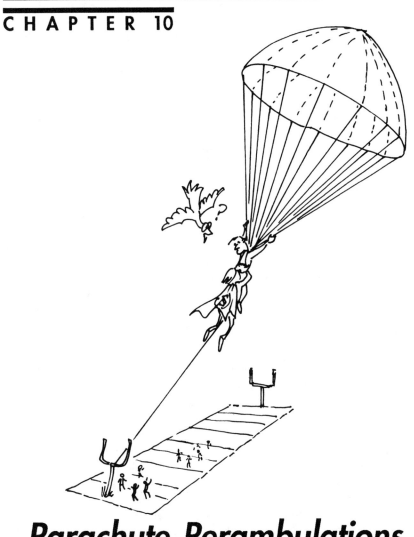

Parachute Perambulations

"*One thorn of experience is worth
a wilderness of warning.*"

James Lovell

In 1972, the fledgling staff at Project Adventure were still creatively casting about, on a day-to-day basis, as to what the curriculum content would be for the following day. It was a heady time of alternating pedagogic panic and satisfying serendipity.

Much of the creative curriculum that appeared each week resulted from recollections of adolescent adventures that I had enjoyed many years earlier. Riding a dragged sled behind a wind-driven parachute, was one of those nostalgic gems (Southern California beaches, c. 1963) that turned out to be well received by sophomore physical education students at Hamilton-Wenham Regional High School.

To make terrestrial wind-riding possible, we obtained a 32′ diameter personnel chute from the local state Government Surplus Agency, bought a triangular metal snow sled, and clipped one to the other with a locking D carabiner.

The land-based "flight" procedure was to pick a spot on the field far enough away from the surrounding trees to allow a steady blow, and to orient the parachute downwind as to receive the incoming flow of air. The flapping edges of the chute were held to the ground by two students until the sled was clipped to the risers. An eager rider then plopped onto the sled, grabbed the two plastic handles and gazed resolutely down field. When all seemed ready, including the often gusting, flukey wind, the two chute controllers picked up the edges of the canopy and allowed the *nylon mushroom* to fill with air.

The brief pre-launch instructions to the rider were to firmly grip the sled's handles unless the parachute itself became airborne. This juncture would be self-evident, because the front of the sled would raise up, sometimes establishing over a 45-degree angle with the ground. At that poignant moment of angled intent, the student was instructed to release his grip with dispatch and roll backward off the sled—like there was a choice! With the rider's weight removed from this unlikely wind-powered vehicle, the billowing chute often lifted the counterbalanced weight of the vacated sled abruptly into the air. If the wind was blowing constantly hard, the sled/chute combination would drift up and over the tree-bordered edge of the field, *never* to be seen again; truly a curriculum event to remember and savor. The loss of the sled and parachute did require, however, that the teacher have some other curriculum gem in mind for the remainder of that chuteless class.

We used up a few parachutes this way, and lost others in the trees, where small branch punctures of the rip-stop nylon became gigantic gaps, as the wind tore at the trapped fabric. To prevent the accelerating chute from bolting into the trees at the end of the field, the remainder of the class (all those not seated on the sled) situated themselves downwind, somewhere toward the estimated direction of the mushroom-like wind sock, and at the last second jumped into and onto the bulbous canopy—a daunting and exhilarating feat, considering the size and speed of that shifting, wobbling wind package. The withered and defeated chute was then grabbed at the top airhole and pulled obediently up-wind back to the starting point. Notwithstanding our regular equipment losses, we continued *field flying* because the activity was so popular with the students and the surplus chutes were reasonably priced.

At about this time I became interested in hang gliding, eventually building a prototype hang glider at the school from a purchased kit. (See *The Plastic Pigeon*.) We never did much with the finished glider from a curriculum standpoint because the student riders (short flights off the sand dunes at Crane's Beach) would predictably oversteer, catch a wing tip in the sand, and snap the aluminum leading edge of the wing. Recognized as the resident *expert*, all the glider repair was designated to my able *expert*ise. After a half dozen wing tips snapped off, I became disillusioned with experimental flight and delegated the final and multi-patched remains of "The Plastic Pigeon" (its wing surface was made of nylon reinforced plastic tarp material—not your high-tech flying machine) to the PA office basement.

I have related all the above vignette material as background for the following high-flying narrative.

On an unusually warm October school day, rather than bringing out the parachute for wind rides on the field that become known as the *flight deck*, I had an on-site inspiration that promised great adventure and the potential of curriculum immortality. As it turned out, my mortality was more at risk.

At the time, Project Adventure was using goldline rope for rock climbing and ropes course use. Goldline was extremely strong and, because it was manufactured of nylon, exhibited a considerable amount of stretch under load. I tied (bowline knot, of course) one end of a 200' length of this rope to a cross section of the high school's football goal post. (The goal post was made of 3–1/2" diameter steel pipe, cemented into the ground; a substantial anchor.) Approaching the other end of the rope down field, I put on the harness that we used for hang gliding and clipped the rope end bowline into the harness. Using another carabiner, I clipped the joined risers of a surplus parachute also into the harness, essentially turning myself into a human kite. The potential for flight soon manifested itself.

With no feelings of trepidation (obscured by the fires of innovation), I instructed the students holding the chute to **"OPEN THE CANOPY"**; I was psyched. The wind quickly filled the billowing nylon, pulling my puppet-like body left and right, as I spontaneously performed a crazy tip-toe dance. After a few seconds of this herky-jerky ballet, I was relieved of my contact with the turf, rising abruptly to a height of perhaps ten feet above the field. The students below me (D block) were ecstatic, cheering my gently swaying body and broad grin. I was experiencing sensory overload, but I do remember looking down at their unbelieving upturned faces, not more than 8–10 feet below me, thinking how happy they appeared. There was no doubt that I had their attention.

Everything was happening the way I had imagined it would. I had thought a lot about trying tethered flight, but up to this point had given no thought as to how I would get down once airborne. I began thinking about it. Before any ideas for controlled descent came to mind, the wind speed picked up, and I experienced an express elevator-like sensation as I was abruptly lifted to about thirty feet (estimated later by a poll of on-site observers). Then the wind died.

Although the chute was mostly inflated, it was located above me at an angle and my body didn't establish enough drop speed to completely deploy the canopy. I hit the asphalt track hard (the running track surrounding the football field was supposed to be rubberized, but . . .), hard enough to sting my heels and knock the wind out of me. As I lay gasping on the heated black surface of the track, my immediate concern was with my stinging feet and lack of breathing; it should have been elsewhere. The wind gusted hard once again, first dragging me across the track and onto the grass, then once again into the air. My concerns immediately prioritized themselves, as I began to appreciate my predicament and the swiftly developing potential for disaster.

One of the student leaders, recognizing that my gasps for help were not chortles of joy, tackled me around the knees as I floated by, then joined me as part of the wind-borne package being propelled and dragged by the powerful gusts.

Fortunately, the remainder of the students reacted heroically to our plight, grabbing us both on the next tack across the field. With close to thirty students holding the bucking chute, I was unclipped, ending my aborted attempt at flight.

As the students (some smiling, some concerned) checked me out, the wind *REALLY* picked up. The parachute, still attached to the rope, reacted like a wild horse in harness to the increased wind pressure and bent that 3–1/2" diameter metal goalpost to nearly a 60 degree angle. If the rope had been connected to my harness, I would have been treated to a view of the football field from close to 100 feet. The descent from that height is best left to conjecture, but in retrospect, I'm just as happy that my bod wasn't up there to test the stopping capacity of that capricious nylon vehicle.

I have told this story many times over the years, because it is both humorous and instructive. The aspect of the narrative that bothers me most, however, and one that I am reluctant to admit, is that if I had made a successful "flight" that day and had been deposited back on the field gently, I'm sure that I would have let one of the students take my place.

CAVEAT—Think your new sure-fire adventures through before putting your body (or anyone else's) on the line.

Denouement

At the time of my fractured flight and soon thereafter, I was more concerned with the horrendous bend that I had caused in the goal-post than in the potential disaster involving my continued existence. I sent the much amused and appalled D Block class back to the school building and awaited the next class, wildly planning how I was going to straighten out that massive bend in the goal post.

With the few minutes that I had between classes, I arranged a truckies' hitch set-up using the 200' rope and a few carabiners. This well-known pulley-like hitch allows almost a 2–1 mechanical advantage to be developed. I figured if 30 high school sophomores would all pull on the end of the rope that was still attached to the goal-post juncture of crossbar and upright, I could multiply their efforts by say 1.7, and maybe duplicate or even exceed the pulling power of the wind. It worked. The goalpost bent satisfyingly backward to almost an upright position. There was a small S shaped bend down near the bottom of the support pole that was destined to be permanent and which caused the crossbar to slant ever so slightly away from the field.

No one said much about the mishap, because that was back when Project Adventure was wallowing in local support and could do no wrong. Not one of the coaches said a thing to me, and I wasn't about to mention the permanent bend.

65

About two years later, during a home football game, the home football team was behind by 1 point and the game was drawing to a close. A field goal would win the game, and the ball was within the kicker's range. The kick was made and the ball bounced off the cross-bar back onto the field. I have no doubt that the slight lean of the goal post caused the ball to hit the crossbar rather than sneaking over. It was at least ten years before I told anyone about what I had done and the story about the missed field goal. I still haven't told the coaches: what the heck, it's just a game.

If you are ever in Hamilton, Massachusetts, take a walk out to the football field behind the high school, and check out the goalpost that is closest to the school end of the field—the bend is still there. If you want to stop by the Project Adventure office in the neighboring town of Wenham you can also check out the bend in my back—it's still there, too.

CHAPTER 11

Oz Waters

"I thought I was in the driver's seat,
but I wasn't even in the car."

Anonymous

The first book that I put together for Project Adventure was an expository extravaganza entitled *Cowstails and Cobras*, a collection of my Outward Bound notes, recollections of useable childhood fun and games, and a written curriculum recording of what had been happening during the formative years at The Project. "Cowstails" outlined and detailed how to build a challenge ropes course, teach games, lead initiative problems, and other pieces of instructional esoteria involved with an adventure curriculum. As it turned out, Project Adventure sold approximately 45,000 copies of CT&C before deciding that there was an uncomfortable amount of outdated information twixt the covers, and summarily canned that particular edition in 1989. (Replaced in 1991 with *Cowstails and Cobras 11*, a substantial rewrite of the original.)

One of those original copies was purchased in 1982 by a *bloke* named Jim Johnson from a bookstore in Tasmania. (Quick—Where in the world is Tasmania? Wrong! Tasmania is an island, one of Australia's seven states, and situated just south of Melbourne, Victoria.) As the result of perusing the book's contents and getting turned on to the infectious and often bizarre activities, Jim decided to contact the book's author and see if he would like to lead a workshop at an outdoor education venue in Queensland, thus offering a hands-on opportunity for Australian teachers to experience what the text promised; "Adventure training that defined compassion, trust, and commitment through jointly experiencing a series of demanding, and exciting activities, and which allowed students to achieve beyond their initial expectations." The author was pleased to accept.

Which is to say that I was headed for Australia to climb a few trees, lead some games, and make people laugh, not a bad anticipated scenario; all in all. The only drawback to the trip (Boston to Queensland) was the 24+ hours of airline coach existence. I'm not really complaining, considering the horrendous rigors and depravation experienced by seagoing First Fleet travellers back in the 18th century, but discomfort is relative, in that released and recycled intestinal gas within a closed metal tube at 35,000 feet is as onerous to the trapped travellers as those fetid olfactory encounters experienced within a secured ship's hold. I've made the Australasian round trip eight times, so there obviously must be something to make the plastic food, cramped seats, stale air, small screen movies, and lack of in-flight pull-up facilities worth the trip. And there is; Australia isn't just a place, mate, it's an experience.

After having facilitated the adventure programming workshop at Pepperina Hill Outdoor Education Center, of which Jim was the director, he and his lovely wife Janis, invited me to their home on the Gold Coast, a beach vacation mecca near the town of Surfer's Paradise in Queensland (I'm not kidding, that's the town's name . . . look it up).

Jim and Janis were the perfect hosts, offering fine Australian wine with scrumptious home-cooked dinners at their hill side A-frame home. Recreation facilities included tennis, local pubs with slot machine bars, skin diving, topless beaches, and *surf ski surfing.*

Rapid rewind to 1954. I spent my early teen years in Hawaii, during which time I didn't do much else except surf and skin dive. (This ebullient time was reflected later in trying to match tested intellectual potential to abysmally low S.A.T. scores.) During those idyllic aqua-oriented years, I developed a water-based comfortability within a wide range of ocean and surf conditions; large waves did not intimidate me.

When Jim mentioned going for a surf in one of his letters, I had responded enthusiastically, perhaps overly so, because when I got there he told me that he had rented a board for me. That presented a problem, because all the surfing I did as a teen wave-basher was on what we called at the time, a Paipo board (now refered to as a Boogie board). A Paipo board then, was a short, thin, slightly curved and beveled plywood board that, held in front of the surfer, measured approximately from mid-section to extended finger tips. A body surfer, wearing fins and half-lying on a Paipo board, could slash down the face of very large swells and usually escape the actual breaking part of the wave by cutting back over the top or "pearling" at the bottom; i.e., attempting to kick back into the wave's base. I loved this kind of breakneck surfing, immersed in and feeling very much a part of the ocean's flow and power. AND, much of this type of surf was near the shore, a brilliant white section of strand inhabited by smooth brown-skinned creatures who applauded our skilled and egotistical *hot curl* maneuvers. I am awash in nostalgic indulgence—the memories are so pleasant and intense that I can practically taste the salt and see (dare I imagine touch?) the *wahines.*

As it turned out, the board Jim had rented was not a surfboard per se, but a board that was indigenous to and typical of the Australian surf scene, a *surf ski;* what a misnomer. This masochistic and ill-named kayak/surfboard half-breed had nothing to do with skiing. Its questionable ergonomic engineering represented a short and narrow surfboard with shallow indentations scooped out on the deck to fit a rider's posterior and heels. Too true! You sat upright on this thing and propelled it with a double-bladed kayak paddle. It even had a buckled automobile-type seatbelt to help hold you onto the board. HA! Double HA!

With all my athletic background and training, including the occupational years I spent working on ropes course challenge balance events, there was no way I was going to surf on this thing. Surf? I couldn't even balance upright without using both paddle blades to flail the water. The double ended paddle was obviously not engineered for propulsion, but for maintaining a vertical breathing position, during which frantic in-balance/off-balance time you hoped the "ski" would float toward shallow water.

During this initial ocean survival phase, I would drop my legs into the water to increase my center of gravity (while gazing seaward, pretending to be looking for the next big wave set), until I realized what my two white Kielbasa-like legs must look like from underneath to *JAWS*. I jerked my legs spasmotically from the water and, disrupting whatever balance I had established, flipped immediately from kind-of-vertical to a horizontal, thrashing get-me-back-on-the-board Shamu position that exposed 2/3 of my white body to all the ravenous, monsters of the sea waiting immediately beneath the board. Flipping over and over on this board-from-hell, reminded me what ropes course participants must feel like after their umpteenth try on the Fidget Ladder (with crocodiles under the ladder).

Eventually I began to develop a feel for the unpredictable movements of the board as it responded to the even less predictable movements of the waves and my herky-jerky balance responses. I was still off the board more than I was topside, but at least now I felt I had a chance for survival. I began to coordinate the paddle thrusts with thoughtful body kinetics and found that a confident abandonment to the situation resulted in better balance and some forward movement, but I still couldn't imagine putting on the seatbelt; I could only visualize its use as a feeding device to hold me in position upside down until the sharks, sensing another vanilla lollipop, had their way with me. (It's well known that certain species of Australian sharks have acute vanilla sensors that allow these animals to beam in on hapless upside-down surfers—it's true.)

Jim, during all this time (firmly belted in), was surfing in on a variety of beautifully formed waves, shouting occasional words of encouragement. He seemed to be enjoying himself immensely; I noticed him laughing a lot.

After we had been out in the ocean for some time, the waves smoothed out and the foaming sets came through less frequently, so I had more time (between white frothed thrashings) to maneuver, navigate, and gain some confidence. At about that time, Jim glided over and asked if I would like to paddle out to where he did some offshore reef snorkeling. Since I had not upended for at least two minutes, I confidently answered yes, thinking that straight line paddling would give me a break from the breakers. We began smoothly paddling directly offshore until after ten minutes or so (and only one upending) we were about a half mile from the beach.

You have to understand that Jim is probably the most at-ease person I have ever seen around or in the water. Even though I was literally brought up near the ocean, and spent hundreds, no, thousands of hours pursuing aquatic sports, I don't have the genetic or perhaps atavistic *vibrations* that allow a oneness with the ocean that Jim has in spades. I'm not even sure he knows he has it. Nonetheless, our brief paddle offshore was a "stroll in the park" for Jim; in fact, he indicated that he often *swam* out to this shallow reef area to dive, rather than encumbering himself with a surf ski. I confidently indicated that I certainly felt the same way, but also didn't mind an occasional paddle.

I was impressed with the area (beautifully clear and warm), with Jim (as above) and peripherally with myself (for being there and remaining upright).

We had been at the reef site for about five minutes and I was becoming more comfortable with the surf ski; actually enjoying myself. Jim had paddled about 50 meters farther off shore when I heard him call back to me, but couldn't understand what he was trying to communicate, even as he shouted. I saw him pointing to my left and beyond where I sat bobbing on the even swells, and thought I heard the word *turtle*. I turned quickly toward the direction of his upraised arm expecting to see either a herd of sea turtles or a large wave about to separate me from my tenuous raft, and . . . SHEeeeIT!!!!!! I heard nothing, but viscerally felt the theme music start (bump-BUMP, bump-BUMP...) as my stop-action visuals flashed the warning, THIS IS NOT A TEST, THIS IS THE REAL THING! Straight out of your classic grade B, bubble-heavy, SCUBA flick a dark grey, perfectly proportioned dorsal fin sliced through the swells toward my plump sausage encumbered "tippy canoe." I felt like bait, veritable human *chum*. How come insects have exoskeletons and we don't? Nice going, God!

The fin did not waver and continued to cut directly toward me. I also remember thinking, *"This isn't a movie."* Too true, mate. I could hear Jim continuing to shout something. (Later he told me that I yelled

71

SHARK!) He was trying to tell me that he was coming over so he could get a better look. SHEeeeeIT!!!!!

The shark was a hammerhead and about 5–6 feet long, not large at all as hammerheads go, but certainly large enough to tweak my adrenalin level beyond surfing endorphins. He/she undulated past the bow of my ski without slowing a beat of its fins, as the hammer eye fixed me with a cold, dispassionate, uninterested glare: I was THAT close. During this brief ships-passing-in-the-night encounter, I balanced atop that ski like I had never balanced before in my life. I was centered to the extreme, my entire being drawn into my ki. If the shark had wanted me, he/she would have had to chomp through some balsa and fiberglass to get at the chosen sausages.

I was irrationally disappointed that the shark was not in the least interested in me as appetizer or entree, continuing on its pelagic way as if I were not there. But Jim *was* interested and he was there, asking where the shark had gone, disappointed that he had not been closer to the encounter. I pointed vaguely out to sea, half expecting him to paddle off in pursuit; paddle in one hand, Nikonos camera in the other.

Still rigidly balanced on the board (feet *not* in the water), I continued to feel extremely vulnerable as previously read tabloid stories of Australian MAN-EATING SHARKS scrolled across my salt-blurred eyes. And where was the hammerhead's mother during all this? I promised myself that if I could make it back to the beach PERIOD, I'd spend the rest of my Australian visit looking for Koalas, Kangaroos, and Wombats; anything that wasn't associated with the abyss.

And I did make it to shore, without upending and with a minimum of trashing, unbelievably completing the last hundred meters ON a wave. I dried off, shared the humorous aspects of the experience with Janis, conducted a personal adventure attitude check, and paddled back out toward where Jim continued cavorting in the waves.

Post Script

The next day, surf conditions were untypically poor, so we visited a more populated beach area to check out the "white pointers" (topless bathers of the distaff variety), and hopefully find some offshore waves. As we carried our surf skis toward the ocean, I made careful note of this quaint cultural sunbathing ethic. Entering the surfless water, we once again headed off shore, paddling strongly and efficiently toward a distant orange buoy that Jim had identified as our goal.

Paddling over smooth waveless water, we made what seemed to be good time, but the buoy's relative distance and size was deceiving.

It took much longer than I had anticipated to reach the buoy, which was considerably larger than I had imagined. I looked back toward the beach for the first time and was shocked at how far off shore we had travelled. Also looking around where we were, I noticed a number of equally large orange floats, separated by a hundred meters or so and positioned as to form a large C arc, from and to the shore. The buoy immediately next to us had large letters stenciled on the far side, so that all I could read was ON, and below that RK.* Before I could paddle around to check out the full printing, Jim suggested that we go for a swim and perhaps dive down to the nets to see if any sharks or rays had become entangled.

WHAT nets? WHAT SHARKS?

Later, I had an interesting insight into why I get myself into so many adventurous situations; I just fall into them, and in this case paddled into one. Once again Jim's supreme confidence in the water had lead me to the edge of a situation that might capture a reader's interest, but didn't go over so well *in situ*.

But, what the heck, Jim was already in the water pretending to be a porpoise, so I hitched my painter to the buoy and slipped into the clear, warm water. (I did **not** flip over!) We had no fins or mask, but Jim indicated that if a large shark or ray were trapped in the net that they would most likely be dead, and would be easy to see because of the strong light penetrating the water. Was I really doing this?

Bending at the waist and gliding down in a bottomless sea was eerie, as the lambent light played fleetingly off the dark grid. Without a mask everything was obviously blurred, but I could easily see Jim's silhouette against the net pulling himself deeper. Much farther below, but paradoxically almost within reach, all the cone-shaped light rays gathered in a glorious display of existential perspective; weird and awesomely beautiful. Thankfully, the only "monster of the sea" entwined in the net that day was what looked like a small ray. We made a number of dives up and down that section of net, but with no trapped leviathans to bolster our egos, I experienced a poignant feeling of insignificance, having only slightly penetrated the top layer of deep, deep water.

It was amazing to me how confident I had become since entering the water; now actually looking for something that I would have fervently

---

*The far side of the buoy read: CAUTION
                        SHARK
                        NET

avoided ten minutes before. Jim's confident presence was obviously the reason.

We swam the short distance back to the tethered surf skis, plopped into our custom concave sit holes and paddled off to other OZ adventures—other land-based adventures, let me add.

I later read that the shark net had been in place for over ten years, and that since its deployment there had not been a shark attack or shark sighting at this popular beach. I didn't notice any statistics about sightings or people devoured while swimming beyond or *below* the nets.

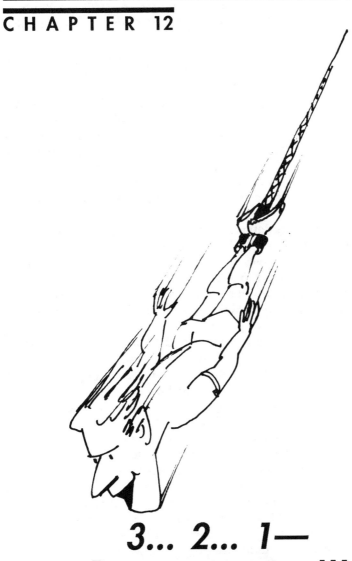

3... 2... 1—
Bungeeeeeeee !!!

"If it's worth doing, it's worth overdoing."
Anonymous

The Scene: August 16, 1990, Berkenhead (Sydney suburb) Australia; approx. 8:15 PM.

I'm seated in a crane cage, with a bondage-like device wrapped tightly around my ankles. A short aussie-type fellow, outfitted in a bizarre jump suit, says supportingly, "When the cage stops swaying I want you to stand up, grab the sides of the door with either hand. I'll say 3, 2, 1—Bungee, and you dive on the word *Bungee.*" This in-depth dialogue was the full extent of my training prior to launching myself head-first toward the lighted harbor surface 130 feet below.

Years ago I had read about ersatz bungee jumping (National Geographic mag—great photos), practiced by intrepid (and vastly uneducated) New Guinea natives. Being somewhat of a cheap thrill aficionado, I was fascinated that this native activity could be "safely" accomplished with such low tech gear; i.e., the jump was made from an unbelievably high and rickety wooden platform with vines tied around the jumper's ankles. To top it all off, the dive was not considered successful (establishing manliness and all that good macho stuff) unless the jumper's forehead made contact with the ground. Perceived danger? *Hoo Ha!* There were admittedly a few mitigating factors such as: the contact area was loose earth that had been "fluffed up," and the drop zone was compassionately situated on a highly angled slope. Also, the vines were tied off (probably a *double granny*) to the platform in a carefully preconstructed area that was designed to break sequentially as the vines tightened. Careful and meticulous engineering like that just makes you want to go out and give it a try, eh?

I was vicariously fascinated nonetheless, and years later was even thinking of giving it a try using goldline rope, but didn't because I was not "vastly uneducated" and my survival instincts were at RED ALERT. When bungee jumping in New Zealand started to get some press a few years back, the thrill factor epicenter of my thalamus (surprisingly, just distal to the survival—fight or flight ganglion) set off those GO FOR IT signals that are hard to ignore. I knew that someday. . .

Someday was August 16., the day before Gloree and I were due to leave Oz for Massachusetts. John Harper (Telecom employee, ropes course fan, and part-time adventurer) and I had been talking about bungee jumping for a couple weeks, because it had just been re-legalized in Australia. Apparently there was a couple months moratorium on the activity as those governmental folks who decide these types of things, thought their thoughts and eventually decided it was OK to role play a yo-yo. So, the evening before I left for the U.S., John and I headed toward Sydney for a pre-dinner leap of faith.

Picture the scene. The jump area is located directly next to a shopping center, and juxtaposes a harbor site, exhibiting lots of moored pleasure boats and gawking shoppers. A large extended crane—looks like a Toys-R-Us knock-off—sits on a section of tarmac (bitumen), next to a brightly painted sign-up shack, festooned with flags and photos. A smiling blonde, sartorially resplendent in a HOT jumpsuit (like hip-HOT, wild pinks, greens, and yellows, etc.) tells me that there is no waiting line: I can see that, and wonder why. She pops me on the scale before I have a chance to exchange pleasantries and tells me that I weigh 14 stones. Is that good I wonder, but not for long, as she inks my hand with some cryptic symbol indicating that 14 stones is apparently just right.

I continue a couple meters to the next station where a competent and tanned young fellow weighs me again and asks me to read the small print disclaimer that they want me to sign. I have forgotten my glasses, so I look at the indecipherable mass of fuzzy black symbols for what seems to be an appropriate length of time, and sign confidently on what appears to be a line at the bottom of the document. Did I just buy a condo in Berkenhead? The smiling fellow quickly files my document and begins arranging my ankle straps; after stamping my hand with another color. The nylon straps buckle on securely and comfortably, finishing off with yet another wrap of velcro. I feel well wrapped and perhaps unjustifiably safe. My hand gets stamped again. My friendly and efficient guide asks me to walk to the crane cage, and I fall immediately to the deck forgetting that my ankles are strapped together; not cool Karl. Regaining my balance and half my cool, I baby step over to and into the cage. I get stamped again, and begin to wonder what the Guiness record is for multiple hand stamps.

Belted into a metal seat, we reach maximum altitude quickly. I've noticed that everything is done quickly, almost too fast to my liking. I find out later that time is money, as one of the employees mentions that they pull in $10,000 on a busy weekend. At $69.00 a pop, that's a lot of jumpers (144.927 wide-eyed yo-yo's to be exact—saves you a trip to the calculator). My bungee mentor checks the color of my wrist band against the color on the bungee cord, and stamps my hand a final time, then asks me to step up to the door, (as above). I try unsuccessfully, recognizing too late that my seatbelt is still tightly wrapped around my waist. Damn, not cool again. My high adventure facilitator apologizes for not undoing the seatbelt, but we both know . . .

From the doorway there's nothing but air twixt me and the water below, and on his BUNGEE signal I'm off, thinking "Try and stamp me now." The initial drop is like missing the Pamper Pole times twenty, but about the time you notice the wind in your ears and the water getting bigger, the bungee rebound trip begins...real fast. Surprisingly, as the bungee provides its braking action, there is very little noticeable pressure on my ankles, and my eyeballs don't feel as if they are going to pop out of my head. In fact, the immediate slowdown and rebound is very satisfying, which isn't saying much considering the free fall alternative. After bouncing up and down about half a dozen times (truly out of control), the crane operator slowly arcs your still gently oscillating body back to the parking lot where a foam mat provides a comfortable touchdown. A back-slapping employee, gushing congratulations about the highly-skilled stunt you just performed, unclips and unvelcros your ankles and the jump is over. Total elapsed time from weigh-in to touchdown, approximately 5 minutes: time is indeed money.

"Nice jump Karl. Here's your certificate, which entitles you to a less expensive jump next time." One's enough, thanks, and I have a plane to catch. The jumpsuit blonde asks me to tell the 15–20 spectators, via a loudspeaker, how much fun it was; being from out of town and all that. I try, but no one steps forward. What I said apparently wasn't very convincing, and $69.00 does buy a lot of groceries.

John takes his jump, rebounds predictably, then joins me for an adrenaline-embellished debrief. We smile, share the good time, and head for dinner; which, if I remember correctly, tasted pretty good.

The trip home the following day, during which time I travelled at 600 mph and looked at the ground from 40,000 feet, was a bit ho-hum. I guess it's all just in your point of view.

CHAPTER 13

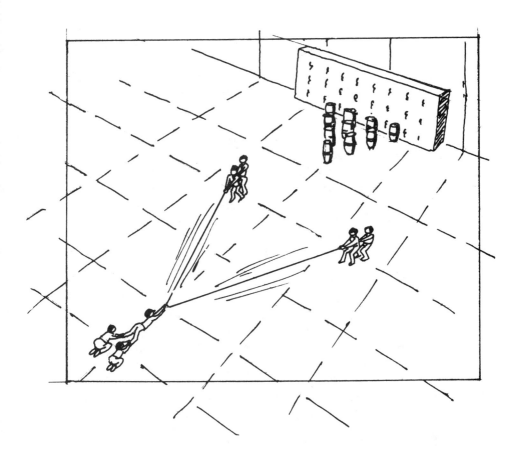

Bungee Cord Shenanigans

"The vitality of thought is in adventure. Ideas won't keep. Something must be done with them."

Alfred Lord Whitehead

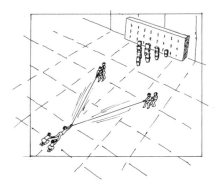

I've been fooling around with Bungee cords ever since I first discovered the old hook & hook type, used to hold gear and treasures secure on a bicycle rat trap rear carrier. I travelled with a special shock cord set each summer during my cranking- out-adventure bike trip peregrinations, and that stretchy cord held, without fail, any odd-shaped road find tucked and stuck behind the saddle. Of course, there are those conservative bikers who would never use an elastic cord to help stow their gear for fear of getting rubber bands wrapped up in their freewheel cogs or receiving a smart whack up 'aside the head by a spontaneously released cord. These were the same guys that coasted downhill, tucked over their drops at 50+ mph . . . and I should worry about getting zinged with a kinetic bungee? But I didn't apply much creative thought to these functional elastic holders, because they did what they were supposed to, if you attached them the way you were supposed to.

It wasn't until I was "fishing" around a surplus outlet in Salem, MA (a warehouse that early Project Adventure staff frequented looking for deals on ropes course building gear) that I found a 75' length of 3/4" diameter bungee cord that looked like it could stop a run-a-way . . . I couldn't think of a run-a-way *what* at the time, but I was sure this heavy duty cord would stop it. Essentially, the cord's adventure potential just appealed to me and I wanted it, so, responding to a seldom-fail sense of "what's-gonna-work-and-be-fun-to-boot", PA purchased the bargain cord for me (couldn't afford not to have it) and I trundled home with a 75 foot stretchy whip for my imagination.

The first thing I did was cut off a section to play with in my back yard, you know something for the kids . . . I needed a limb, and fortuitously a large maple tree was located behind the house near a sizeable blank section of lawn. Years earlier, I had suspended an old lawnmower handle from a substantial overhead limb so that it hung temptingly over the fall-on-me grass. The lawnmower handle provided a dandy swing trapeze and required from the swinger that they use some arm power rather than just settin' in a swing or danglin' from a tire. My two boys enjoyed and used that old lawnmower handle more than any expensive bike or toy purchased for them.

80

To implement my rebound inclinations, I simply replaced the swing rope with a section of bungee cord, knotted the end, and asked the equipment testing experts (my sons) to do something fun with it. They looked at it suspiciously (both liked the lawn mower handle a lot, and thought that it was gone for good), pulled on it a bit and were generally unimpressed with the kinetics or potential. Assuming my catalytic professional mode, I showed them how they could hold the end and bounce around in a substantially expanded circle with minimum ground contact. They thought this was cool and called it *moonwalking*, but the novelty wore thin quickly and requests for the lawn mower handle to be reinstalled became more frequent . . .

I was wondering how I could expand the moonwalking to make it more dramatic, hence thrilling, when I thought of Swiss seating (a type of tied harness) the boys, attaching them to the end of the knotted bungee and launching them from one side of a substantially expanded circle to the far side. It worked like this. I would clip (carabiner) one of the boys into the end of the bungee (bowline loop, of course) and draw them to the outside of the premeasured rebound arc. On release, he (#1 or #2 son) would rebound to the far side of the circle circumference, then immediately recoil back until the kinetics diminished via friction, gravity, ground contact, etc. With nothing in between to slow their passage, you might suppose this marginally out-of-control ping-pong action might be fun, and, of course, it was. This was called *Moon Launch* by the boys (5 & 8 years old) and for a few weeks, boinging back and forth took first place over the lawn mower handle.

During this innocuous play time I was inadvertently gaining experience in use of the bungee and learning a bit about its rebound characteristics. I was also impressed by how tough this stuff was. The exterior, woven nylon mantle protected the scores of internal parallel rubber fibers. That backyard bungee section was not taken in each night or treated respectfully in any way, and at the weathering end of six months, I had developed a high opinion of the product and the manufacturer, whoever that was.

Even having cut off a chunk of bungee for backyard R&D use, I still had a good long section left. I have to admit though, the remaining cord sat around for a couple years in a back storage room waiting for me to get creative. During that time, however, I did cut off a couple short sections for use as trapeze suspenders; scenario and consequence as follows.

One of the indoor ropes course events that Project Adventure regularly installs in gymnasiums is a platform dive to a suspended trapeze. (Yes, this type of circus activity *does* have curriculum purpose, but I just don't have it in my fingers to hit the proper validity keys . . .

again. Drop me a note, and I'll send you a standard response batch of supportive adventure curriculum information that will assuage the fears and bolster the trust of even the most tentative parent and/or administrator.) In one of Boston's suburban schools, I had befriended the physical education teacher and convinced him that use of bungee cords as a suspension system for the trapeze would cause less "shoulder shock" for the students as they dove and grabbed the bar. At this particular middle school gymnasium, in order to connect with the overhead supporting I-beams, I had to remove quite a few square sections of drop ceiling tile. It was difficult work, but the construction results were solid if not aesthetic: a cosmetic disaster, actually.

I attempted the first dive from platform to trapeze (a builder's moral obligation); an easy jump because of my height. I grabbed the trapeze firmly with both hands then dropped waaaay down, rebounding a couple times before the two extended bungee support cords brought me to a stop. I yelled down to my belayer that I was ready to let go and be lowered via the belay rope to the gym floor. This was kind of humorous, because with the stretch of the cords I was only a couple feet above his head. When I let go, to be lowered gently to the floor, the released trapeze fired toward the ceiling with the speed of an arrow, disintegrating two of the remaining drop ceiling tiles like clay pigeons on a skeet range. Needless to say, that was the first and last use of that kinetic trapeze arrangement. The teacher is still my friend.

Taking advantage of my backyard successes (and minimizing the trapeze fiasco), I took the remainder of the bungee cord to a local civil defense fire/rescue practice tower that Project Adventure used occasionally with workshop groups for teaching various rope skills, including rappeling. The 40' wooden tower was enclosed, and had a number of conveniently located, no-glass, large windows for rapid (sometimes not-so-rapid) egress. Just above the top floor window there was a 6" × 6" beam protruding from the building, much like what you would expect to see above an old barn's hay window. We had used this substantial beam in the past for attachment of a rappel rope, so the somewhat logical adventure extension was to attach the bungee cord and take a rebound jump out a window, which I did.

There were three windows, one on each floor of the tower. I tried a jump from the first window (about 10' from sill to ground) hand-holding the bungee cord, and was rewarded with a swift ride to the turf with precious little rebound. So, logically I moved up to the next window and jumped from a greater height (20') to give the bungee more opportunity to stretch and rebound. The stretch was obviously there, as I hit the ground with a fair impact, but the rebound was still *sorely* lacking. I let go of the well-stretched cord, but not fast enough, as the mantle zipped across my bare palms reminding me that gloves have a purpose other than keeping your fingers warm.

Rather than illogically moving up to the third window, I decided to let someone else experience some of this return-to-the-earth fun and offered the cord to a smaller, lighter person. As it turned out, that individual did not feel comfortable just holding onto the cord, so we compassionately tied up a harness arrangement, and were rewarded with a jump and rebound that more closely fit what we had in mind; in fact the jumper almost rebounded back into the window from which she had jumped. This "almost" accomplishment gave us something to strive for, and for the next dozen jumps, various smaller people tried their best to re-enter the exit window.

Larger people recognized that they were obviously at a performance disadvantage (having watched me slam into the ground), and were perfectly happy to maintain a *firma* foundation, saying supportive things like, *"Oooh, nice try; you only missed by a few inches."* or *"You're perfect for this jump, go for it!"* However, perfect or not, none of the jumpers made it back into an exit window, until my son Matthew gave it his try. You have to remember that Matt was a veteran jumper, having logged many "moon shots" on his backyard launcher. Bungee jumping held no fears for this young fellow, as he smilingly positioned himself in the window for the leap. However, as it turned out, at 8 years old he didn't have enough mass to produce much of a rebound, so his jump, although entertaining to him and the heavyweights below, caused him to just bounce around without ever making ground contact. To a lad this age, bouncing around willy-nilly is an end in itself, but the task-oriented adults in attendance wanted a window re-entry, so they asked Matt if he minded being launched from the ground. As long as more bouncing was involved, he was enthusiastically ready.

It didn't take long to discover just the right amount of bungee pull to produce a direct window hit. Amidst much cheering and backslapping, Matt recorded an adventure first (bungee jump window re-entry) that would look good on any resumé.

It wasn't too long after the window jumping escapade that I discovered the joys and excitement of The Human Slingshot.

We had been fooling around in workshops with something called a *Funnelator*, actually just a surgical tubing slingshot arrangement used for propelling water balloons great distances. Appreciating the simplistic V-vector mechanics of this primitive launching device didn't require a degree in propulsion engineering, so, imbued with the fires of innovation and sparked by the lure of unknown adventure, we laughingly set up the world's first (maybe the second) human slingshot.

We had the launch mechanism (bungee cords), and we had the volunteer (me), all that was needed was a means of cutting down on friction, and gym scooters provided the rolling answer. Here's the launch mode scenario. The rider lies ventral down on top of two gym scooters, one scooter located at about pelvis level and the other at chest height. An 80' length of 5/8" diameter bungee cord is held in the middle (40' mark) with both hands by the rider. Each knotted end of the bungee is held by two committed pullers—total of four pullers. The bungee at this juncture looks like a giant V, with the rider at the bottom (apex) of the V. You also need two people to hold onto the feet (one each) of the rider. Beginning to get the picture? Check out the cartoon at the beginning of this essay.

Here's when the potential builds to kinetic. The launch area, of necessity, is situated at one end of a gym or field house, so that the rider is oriented down court, ensuring ample acceleration and riding space: we'll cover deceleration soon. The pullers begin to stretch the bungee cord by jogging away from the rider on the two V vectors. All four pullers must do this concurrently and swiftly.

As the bungee begins to stretch, the rider **must** hold on with great determination, and the foot-holders must do the same. When the pullers believe that they have reached the potential stretch limit of the cord, one of them shouts, **"RELEASE!"** At this command, the two foot-holders let go immediately and simultaneously (the rider, at this juncture, does **NOT** release) and the rider manifests the bungee's stretched potential with immediate acceleration.

Imagine all the aircraft carrier movies you have seen, surfeit with air craft catapult-launching scenes from the deck; it's like that, and to the rider (face to the floor), even faster. When the bungee has spent its pull potential, the rider casts the spent cord over his/her rapidly-moving horizontal person, and continues speeding toward the down court destination, usually the wall at the other end of the basketball court. To prevent injury, gym pads are preliminarily arranged along the expanse of target wall. Use padding liberally as this bizarre humanoid slingshot arrangement is predictably not very accurate.

If the rider misinterprets the *RELEASE* command above, and lets go of the bungee prematurely, two things happen very rapidly: the released cord whistles menacingly though the air, and the pullers fall down (a simple description of retro-catapulting). This slam-bang scenario does not engender trust; try to not let it happen by continually reminding the nervous rider to *hold on tight*. As the participants become used to the commands and the "feeling" of this activity, pull and release mistakes are less common, and less spectacular.

The rider must keep his/her eyes open to anticipate the approaching wall, and to know when to drag a foot to both slow momentum and to turn his/her body sideways. A side body approach is necessary to provide the largest expanse of anatomy to hit the pads.

For advanced (more than one attempt) riders, the activity of *human pinball* offers a skill orientation to the ordinary straight shot toward the wall. Ask your rider to wear a helmet, then after the launch and the overhead casting of the cord, indicate that he/she must hold their arms next to their body. This arms-at-the-side narrow profile is necessary to prevent illegal knocking down of the lightweight plastic bowling pins that have been arranged down court in the typical pyramid style reminiscent of normal bowling. The highest skill level dictates that only those pins knocked over by helmet contact can be counted. Truly, a game for advanced bungee riders only.

Of course, sling shotting people along a flat smooth surface was bound to encourage zip wire (flying fox) launches. Many of you, I'm sure, are familiar with zip wire pulley descents off a high challenge ropes course. The retro idea here is to shoot people UP the zip wire, and then let them ride comfortably down to the normal bungee brake set up. This works! It's been done, and the beauty of the situation is that the rider cannot go off course or run into anything.

Now, let me tell you about some things NOT to do with bungee cords.

• If two of your friends hold a section of bungee cord between them at about waist level, and back away from one another until the cord becomes semi-taut, it is not a good idea for another person to run at the cord (a la TV wrestling antics) to test its rebound capabilities. Rest assured, it rebounds well, which your pliant bod does **not** as it hits the turf going backwards doing mach 1.4.

• If two of your friends hold a section of bungee cord between them and back away from one another until the cord becomes semi-taut (sound familiar?) the temptation might present itself to let go of the ends simultaneously to see if the bungee can rebound against itself, causing a dramatic spaghetti-like collapse of the kinetic cord halfway between the two gamblers. If one person is slightly (less than half a second) inattentive he/she will be visited by a winging/zinging living and abusive get-away-from-me mass of hard hitting bungee. This is to be avoided.

• If you want to "shoot" one of your friends into a pool, make sure you aim them down the length of the pool, **NOT** the width. Actually, it's

85

probably a better idea not to launch your friend into a pool at all. Further details withheld so as not to upset the reader's sense of the author's commitment to safety.

• If you attach a 100 foot length of 1/2" or 5/8" bungee cord to a tree trunk, and then pull the other end away from the tree trunk, you are developing the potential for an explosive kinetic recoil. By backing a *couple hundred feet* away from the tree and releasing your end (the other end is tied to the tree, remember?), the bungee recoils toward the tree with great speed, picking up bits of grass, twigs, dirt, and finally multi-whacking the trunk with the undiminished whistling flight of a brobdingnagian length of rubber linguini. This all occurs in less than 2 seconds. Impressive! If someone thinks about standing next to the trunk to see if they can get out of the way in time . . . that's not a good idea. The nightmarish approach of the "living" cord is impressive, as is the sound of its arrival.

• Do NOT use any length or diameter or combination of bungee as a substitute for a belay rope, **PERIOD**.

CHAPTER 14

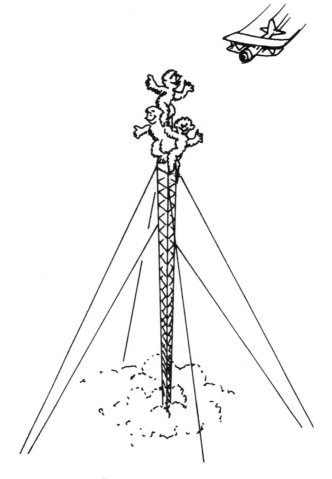

The Tower

*"To enjoy the flavor of life, take big bites.
Moderation is for monks."*

Lazarus Long

haven't played *Sardines* for a couple years. It's not a bad game all in all, but lately I avoid it. Looking for a hidden someone to hide with in a darkened house or gymnasium just doesn't do it for me anymore. Maybe it's the late hour (the game is seldom suggested before 11 PM), or perhaps the fact that the hider is often so motivated to not be found that he/she usually isn't . . . I don't know. But, our workshop group had just finished a late bout of *Sardines* at the yearly Renbrook School BAT (Basic Adventure Training), clinic and the group was breaking up for bed, snacks, talk and even a couple one-on-one, play-til-you-puke games; some of these workshop people are hardcore—and young.

Sully (workshop participant) had grabbed his cane and was gimping toward the gym door, as Nicki (co-instructor) put on her jacket, yawned and also headed in that direction—toward home and the sack. We shared 11:35 PM banalities, and shifted toward our nightly shut-down routines. Someone said it. I'm not sure if it was me, but someone mentioned the TV Tower. . . . The voice within echoed **TV TOWER!**: I was awake.

I've been looking at that narrow and immensely tall structure for over five years, experiencing each time a blend of fear, awe, and unsettled attraction. Fear is a pedagogic tool I use occasionally as part of my adventure curriculum bag of tricks, toward trying to convince people that they can perform beyond their perceived boundaries. Programmed fear (perceived risk) is a useful tool, so I use it, but seldom experience it. I'm reluctant to admit it, but the tower may represent more fear than I want to face, perhaps more than I think I can handle. Can I admit to that? A friend of Nicki has climbed it . . . Sully climbed it . . .

THE TOWER . . . Jesus, they are talking about climbing **THE** Tower. The bantering comments are almost too casual, too convincing; "When are we going to do it?" "Sure would be fun to do it on a moonlit night." "Karl, can you make it down this way on the next full moon?" "Sure (never happen) but we have half a moon tonight, why don't we just go do it now?" AArgh! Did I say that? They look at each other. They agree. Oh Shit, I'm agreeing, too. Done. Sully suggests, "Get your stuff together and let's go. We can be back here by 3 AM." I think of his hip joint operation—the cane—Nicki's recent shoulder operation: Christ, I'm in one piece, I can do this. Sure I can do this. Let's go!

Adrenalin has picked up the pace. The workshop group is gearing down as we frenetically shift into overdrive. I grab a jacket for the inevitable breeze and coolness at the TOP. Positive thinking: I feel good about that. I choose my safety webbing color with care—red—it shows black in the night. My *Rambo* inclinations continue as I change into blue and black clothing. If I had face camouflage I'd probably use it. This nocturnal exercise in fear fulfillment is obviously not legal, so comments between us become conspiritorial and self-conscious. One of the workshop participants asks what we're doing, where are we going? With a half-smile I reply casually, "Climbing," and take some satisfaction in his exclamation of disbelief and awe.

I realize something, as the three of us scuttle about making our personal preparations, an insight that greatly amuses me—this is play, serious play, but play nonetheless. Three adults getting ready to do something benignly illegal and dangerous in the middle of the night: perfect. Sixth grade memories of emulating Batman sneak grinningly into my quasi-adult reveries. No bat cape tonight Robin; strangling on a snarled ersatz shoulder cover would not be cool.

Sully parks his car 1/4 mile from the entrance to the access road and warns us that while we are walking back that quarter mile, to make sure we don't look like three people who are planning to climb a thousand foot TV tower. I nod knowingly, not knowing at all what he means. I'm now convinced that the occasional car zipping by in the dark has at least one passenger who comments, "Well, there go another three for the tower."

Finally, the access road. A quick right turn, and the grade increases. Our necks crane to watch the tower strobe lights flash in sequence to the top. Awesome. The twin towers have their jack-in-the-beanstalk earth contact within a few hundred meters of where we stand. Our strides shorten and become more purposeful. I'm getting warm.

The tower we are targeted to climb is just over 1,000 feet high. The adjacent tower, reputedly protected by an alarm system, measures over 1,300 feet to the top. I fully and passionately believe the second tower is wired and don't begrudge the 300 extra feet at all. The sequential and metronome-like flashes of the strobe lights provide a surreal effect to an already other-worldly atmosphere. We continue steadily and silently up the road toward the base of the tower. This is night maneuvers; this is the REAL THING. I'm psyched.

We pause in the low concealing undergrowth to arrange harnesses, pelvic wraps, and psyche. I'm the only one using webbing, so

Sully and Nicki buckle up and are ready before I'm half wrapped. The level of conversation is almost non-existent, but then this IS a clandestine night operation and what's to talk about immediately prior to climbing a thousand foot ladder?

Outfitted, we head for the chain-link fence that surrounds our goal. I concentrate on not breaking branches with my steps, convinced that the twenty-four hour SWAT team assigned to these towers is listening for just that type of audial trespass. The fence itself is only about eight feet tall. Three strands of barbed wire on top make the initial climb only slightly more difficult and in fact, eventually easier since the barbed strands are strung horizontally parallel. Standing on the top barbed strand allows us to reach up and grab a section of the tower superstructure that would have otherwise been out of reach. Sully leads off, then Nicki and I follow. From the fence it's a couple easy moves to the base of the ladder which, in the dark, is by far the longest I've ever not seen. Without any fanfare Sully is off (his halting cane-aided step on the ground is nonexistent on the ladder—this gives me pause) Nicki looks down at me, smiles wanly and follows into the vertical night.

Sully indicated earlier that we should climb the first 100 feet quickly because of the well-lighted area at the bottom of the tower: perfect target for the diligent SWAT teams. Banging out those first couple hundred rungs helped dispel any thoughts about stopping before you started. Our first few frantic minutes of climbing were involved only with stepping, grabbing (God, did I grab), and hard breathing. "This is easy. We're cruising. What was I worried about?"

A cross-section of the tower itself represents almost a perfect square. Inside that approximate 6–7 foot square, the humongously long ladder we were climbing was attached kitty-corner to one of the interior right angle corners. If you wanted to (I wanted to), you could have squeezed into the space between the ladder and the right angle of the tower superstructure, but climbing would have been difficult, if not occasionally impossible. Climbing inside the tower allowed no protection except for the feeling that you were at least enclosed within something: small consolation. I was content (content is not the right word in this context) to be where I was, in contrast to climbing the OUTSIDE of the tower. Talking about this later, we speculated what would have happened if one of us had disengaged from the ladder. I'm glad we talked about it *later*. Immediately behind me was a 6" diameter PVC pipe that, as it turned out, continued all the way to the top. I assume that wires of some kind were encased within this pipe. I mention the pipe only because it gave me some assurance that I could reach out behind me (if I held on with one hand) and touch something. Seems like a nothing something as I write this, but at the time. . .

We stopped at about 200 feet for a rest. At the rest stops we clipped our harness-attached carabiners to the ladder or a piece of the superstructure. During the climb I NEVER put my weight on the safety system, but knowing it was there definitely increased my sense of security. Since I was at the bottom of our climbing trio, Sully and Nicki usually moved off the ladder and stood on a cross section of the tower during rest stops. Fortunately, every 20' or so, there were right-angled structural pipes adjacent to the rungs that I could stand on without having to give up the ladder. Standing on these pipes during rest stops allowed me to look directly down between my legs . . . God! The developing tunnel-like perspective was unreal.

I was still feeling good, even after having looked down past my toes at the perspective that 200 feet of vertical triangulation allowed. The ladder visually broke up the interior square of the tower and formed an internal triangle that yawned twixt my legs. I could make out the tower's base because of the lights below, but all I could see as I looked up was the ladder disappearing into the night and, depending upon my positioning, occasionally the bottom of Nicki's boots.

During this first rest stop, I wrapped my arms through and around the ladder and, resting my chin on a rung, briefly admired the half moon rising, the myriad lights of the city, and the individual pin-pricks of light that differentiated the homes and stores. I wasn't thinking of how much farther we had to go (800+ feet), only where I was and what I was experiencing. It was undeniably a NOW moment.

We shared a couple mandatory comments, "How ya doin'?" "Feel OK?" "Great view, eh?" and started climbing again. I was *really* concentrating on the climb, specifically the ladder and where I was putting my hands and feet—particularly my hands. I have always trusted the strength in my arms, so the positioning of each separate grip on the ladder was of consuming interest.

It was quite dark now, the light from below having lost all illuminating power. Doubts began creeping into my mind; fear actually. I concentrated even harder on the ladder, I saw nothing else. I watched my hands wrap around each rung/rail connection, fascinated by my strong yet fragile connection to the ladder; I could let go, I could faint . . . Can't afford these thoughts; think of only hand and foot placement on the ladder. And I do, so intently that I miss the first strobe light entirely. Of course, the strobe flashes outward, but even so I should have at least noticed it: a fleeting disappointment.

Sully calls from above that we are nearing the half-way point. The tower construction plans apparently called for some heavy-duty beams and bolting at this mid-juncture, not only providing an obviously strong structural joint, but a morale boost, and butt rest for your intrepid evening climbers. The view of the countryside from 500+ feet is less than magnificent considering that I can't see much of it in the dark, but I'm pleased to be here, in fact, too pleased. Reaching the halfway point had become too satisfying. Sitting somewhat comfortably on the smallish cross beam, I rationalize the next 500 feet as being very much like the first half, so what's the use? I could just sit here and wait for Sully and Nicki to return; I don't even have to get out of their way. It's not cold, the view is OK and I might even have a profound thought or two. After a couple of minutes Sully and Nicki move out . . . I follow.

About 100 rungs above the half-way point, a wave of panic begins and washes over me. For no reason (except for the fact that I'm over 600 ft. up on a skinny tower with no *pro*) I feel weak, anxious, and dizzy. The purpose of gaining the top vanishes as I clip in and call to Nicki that I have to "rest." I fight the feeling, and with a sense of purpose begin climbing again within 30 seconds. I'm OK . . . I'll make the top.

The last set of guy cables disappears below me and I hear Sully announce that we have reached the top. Indeed we have, because suddenly there's no more ladder, just my climbing partners huddled on a 7' × 3' steel grid platform. I scramble aboard, diligently attach my umbilical protection, and join in the subdued celebration. The view from the top is like the view from half-way times 2, and in the surrounding dark not all that impressive. However, I am impressed with myself for having committed to the climb, with Nicki for having overcome a considerable amount of pre-climb doubts, and perhaps most of all with Sully for having made the climb with a bum leg. Having done a lot of crazy and exciting things with friends over the years, I have no illusions about this being a bonding, spiritual experience for the three of us, but I'm happy and satisfied to be here with my two nocturnal climbing partners.

Interestingly enough there has been no noticeable sway either during the ascent or while sitting on the top. The thick and numerous guy wires do their job well. There is about a 10–15 mph wind blowing and the air is cool, but not cold. I speculate aloud about the potential sway effect of a New England nor'easter while looking down at the tiny speck of light over 1,000 feet directly below my posterior . . . Sully mentions having made this climb in a snow storm the previous winter, and during that time estimated the wind velocity at 50 knots. "Not much sway even then" he says, "cold tho," definitely a master of understatement.

We look around, share a few how-do-you-feel observations, and decide it's time to descend, as we are cooling off rapidly. I lead going backward. Having lost count of the number of rungs on the way up, I am determined to count them accurately during the descent.

Climbing down was unremarkable except that it took considerably longer than I had anticipated. The climb to the top took us about 45 minutes including rest stops; the trip down, about 40 minutes. The descending climbing rhythm was different, harder to regulate somehow. I misstepped a number of times (nothing to speak of really), but eventually got used to the akwardness and made it part of the routine: doing anything repetious a thousand times becomes somewhat routine no matter where you are.

We descended 200 rungs, rested, backed off another 200, etc., etc., until we were down and done. There were a total of 1,043 rungs, plus or minus a few. At one point during a rest stop, I tried to estimate the distance between ladder rungs; 12" from rung to rung seemed close. The entire climb was well over 1,000 ft., and that was enough for me.

We descended from the tower via the barbed wire route, took off our gear, and retraced our steps down toward the car. During our quiet walk back, I glanced frequently over my shoulder to watch the strobe's 1,000 foot flash sequence. The old mountaineer's story came to mind about the sadness of having to eventually leave the summit, but also of how that sadness was mitigated by having been there and knowing what the top was like.

I smiled ferociously in the dark.

CHAPTER 15

Rock Running

*"We play for the sake of the game, for play itself. In
this manner, we participate in the essence of existence."*
George Leonard

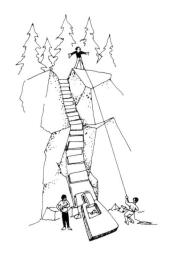

Project Adventure, Inc., has been using a local climbing area in Gloucester (Red Rock) as an instructional venue for rappeling and basic climbing since 1973. Its 70′ comfortably-angled granite face has been the site for many first time rock thrashers, who have frantically wondered how this thin air experience relates to *an innovative and personally rejuvenating adventure education program.*

Just about smack dab in the middle of the conveniently located granite rock face is a lay back flake called **The Zipper**, an unavoidably attractive climbing route that provides the only reasonable (5.5)* ascent for normal people. To the left and right of The Zipper, are 5.10 and above climbs, de rigueur for sticky rubber shoe folks with a sac full of chalk, but for most of us Nike-shod, sweaty-palmed, gimmie-a-bucket climbers, the 5.5 center flake is *the* center of interest. So much so, that after a few times up and down this obvious route, interest wanes, and what-are-we-going-to-do-now? Years ago, variations of the route were tried by instructors, one of which involved getting to the top ASAP, and *rock running* was born. (Other variations at that time included climbing and rappeling clothed only in cardboard boxes, climbing in tandem; i.e., two people on a rope, climbing blindfolded and a couple stunts that are best left unreported.)

The first few speed attempts were in the 30+ second range, usually attempted by staff toward the end of a workshop climbing session when the students were winding down. I can remember when 20 seconds was considered very quick, in fact, we initially boasted of an "under 20 club" to which only the elite could claim membership. People who had struggled for over 5 minutes to reach the top were duly impressed by an under 20 second climb, and so were we.

Early rock runs were hindered by inefficient belay techniques (the belayer couldn't keep up with the climber), no chalk, and lack of *real* climbing shoes. Some of the original sneaker-wearing speed climbers

---

5.5, or any of the decimal numbers included in this article refer to the Yosemite Decimal System (YDS) for determining the relative difficulty of a particular rock climb. Using this system, a 5.0 climb is the easiest, and currently a 5.14 b is the most difficult. Having a graded system allows people to determine which climb is the best suited for their skill level; i.e., easy enough to preclude frustration, but difficult enough to provide a realistic challenge.

included Steve Butler, Charlie Harrington, Nicki Hall (current woman's record holder at 14+ secs.), and Jim Grout. Other interns and occasional trainers also made their attempts, but serious speed "runs" didn't occur until Sept. 2, 1991.

On that day (a Sunday), I got a call at home from one of our international trainers asking if I would like to join a group going to Red Rock and be part of the attempt at setting a new **Zipper** record. How could I say no; the weather was perfect, time was no problem, the format was definitely FUNN, and I had held the record for the past six or so years. That carefully honed record (13.21 secs.—the number had become a permanent part of my memory bank) was not only bested, it was SMASHED.

The very fast times recorded on that Sunday I'm sure were due in part to the use of smearable rubber climbing shoes, copious amounts of chalk, a rear tie-in technique combined with a double person slingshot belay, and a brand of visceral/vocal support that is seldom experienced or heard at Red Rock or *any* climbing venue; the cheering and audial prodding had to be worth at least half a second. Some of the local climbers, also pitting themselves against the somewhat off-vertical challenges at Red Rock, were not enthralled by what was obviously an international crowd having so much irreverent, boisterous fun; playing and competing at what should have been a serious and existential approach to self-awareness and personal limits.

Come on, Rich, explode off that start! Ross, don't hesitate at the crux-reach left and go, go, go! It's right foot high, left foot up, then lunge—don't think mate, just thrash.

Truly a day to remember, friends enjoying a challenge and one another. The record that held for six years (13.21 secs.) was substantially bettered. The new standard (9.33 secs.) is phenomenal, but no need to wait another six years to have a go, and as indicated above, there's lots of records to go 'round: if you want a record, we've got a category. (**The Zipper** climb measures about 60 feet high, with an approximate 80 degree climbing angle.)

97

CHAPTER 16

PA ROADIE

"If you are a rock climber, your friends probably regard you with suspicion. Any form of striving that once made people heros—any quest that carries acceptance of risk—now makes them crazies. To sustain comfort, we have to be safe—safe from confrontation with other people, objects or elements. In a comfortable world the hard edges have been padded, rounded or smoothed—it's the home of the foam-rubber lawn mower. But where there is no risk there is no achievement."

Reader's Digest

I had the brochure in my desk for well over a year, and had been thinking about it a lot longer, but that's how experiential wish lists go, more contemplation than action. I wanted to do something exciting, but was ambivalent about the event, how far I wanted to travel, if I wanted to do it alone, etc. The only thing I was sure of was that I didn't want to travel *north* (cold country) to accomplish whatever adventure presented itself.

I opened my desk drawer a few months ago, searching for something that had escaped my meticulous filing system, and as the result of frantic paper shuffling, the colorful flyer for *Kitty Hawk Kites* glided smoothly to the floor and landed in an open position, displaying tanned, fit, smiling people doing exciting airborne things amidst a panoply of brightly-colored, sun-lit hang gliders. I completely forgot what I was looking for, as this veritable omen of promised flight potential once again stimulated my why-am-I-here-and-not-there psyche manipulators. (For those with a BS bent for science, the manipulators represent a synaptic congruence between the hormonal and pituitary glands, a veritable antipodal synergistic medical paradox, if you know what I mean.)

Not in the least misty-eyed, I reminisced, dragging up seventeen-year-old memories about aborted and unfulfilled hang gliding scenarios from those early days when *Project Adventure* was experimenting with cheap thrills and their application to a vapid . . . I mean valid, curriculum. During those early experimentation days I had purchased a hang gliding kit, spent untold hours constructing it, very little time learning how to fly it, and even less time repetitively crashing it amidst the dunes at Crane Beach. My dreams of unfettered flight were definitely fettered.

This gaily-colored and seductively composed *flyer* on my floor was programmatically promising that flight was yet possible in the sand hills of Kitty Hawk, North Carolina. How could I doubt them, the flyer was obviously well done and Kitty Hawk was steeped in flight tradition; ref. the Wright Brothers' 1903 successful experiment with powered flight.

Planning details zapped through my reveries like a Force 10 kite slicing a Trlby's tail. Who could I get to go . . . ? Operating under the premise that there are still adventurers at Project Adventure I simply asked some of the staff and was pleased that a comfortably sized coterie of like-minded folks were up for the 15-hour drive and the proposed hang gliding lessons.

As we waited and worked on Thursday, fully believing that we would depart from The Rail (in-house vernacular for the PA office building) at an hour prior to the less fortunate stay-at-home programmed adventurers, events of a non-critical nature dictated leaving after 5:00 PM. No sweat, we'll make it up by taking fewer bathroom stops, and who's in a hurry anyway? Our vehicle's only drawback (actually an adjunct to humor) was its non-burping gas tank that took a full 20 minutes to fill. **Scenario**—Pulling into a service station in the early AM, "Yeah, what can I get you?" "Twenty minutes of regular, please."

We cruised through MA, CT, NY, NJ, DE and VA, trading off the driving chore at two-hour intervals and then attempting to sleep amidst various other strangely contorted bodies and boards—that's **SURF BOARDS, DUDES**: radical man, just excellent, pure filth, hang ten, kiss the curl . . . We had in residence a host of wannabies, delivering a stream of Beach Boys lingo while thumbing through and underlining the latest radical tubular moves and sweet young things in the rag mag SURFER TODAY. We couldn't surf, but after 700 miles, we sure knew our way around the culture and the jargon. What the heck—as one of our flaxen-haired female road warriors so astutely pointed out, ". . . here you are in a van with two gorgeous blondes, surf boards, and a six pack headed for a surfing mecca." Hey pardner, it just don't get much better than this!

The van arrived at Kitty Hawk early that next AM, and so did the sun. We taped our eye lids open, had some grits and java, found the Realtor, found the beach house, parked, and headed for the ocean not more than 30 yards across the road and beyond the sandy strand. We reveled in our new digs, the warmth, the beach, and the anticipation of doing *funn* stuff with fun people.

The well appointed rental had multiple bedrooms and baths, and a master bedroom with a full mirrored JACUZZI, which everyone immediately piled into in order to establish a new house record.

That afternoon we checked out Kitty Hawk Kites as to student flight times (they are the largest hang gliding school in the world) and also when the stunt kite competition would be held, ostensibly the two reasons why we were there. Everything was scheduled for mañana, so we shopped around a bit, (checking out the inevitable and seemingly endless panoply of T-shirts and kite paraphernalia), watched the hang gliding classes in progress (not impressive), and did some memorable dune jumping.

Returning to our rented house, we watched a *hukilau* fish netting operation on the sand directly in front of our beach digs. The horseshoe-shaped gill net caught literally thousands of fish, enough to fill the bed of the netter's pick up truck. They also inadvertently gilled an eight-foot thresher shark, a large-toothed genus known for having on rare occasions gobbled various sections of human anatomy—*and* it was caught where we were frolicking in the surf earlier; not bad for a little unprogrammed adventure.

So there we all stood, arms crossed, feet firmly planted in the sand, contemplating the beached shark, commenting on its size, girth, sandpaper skin, and oral capacity when someone suggested an *in situ* exploratory dissection. Knives flashed, with Tim's Spyder-Co blade taking the lead, then executing a beautiful lateral abdominal incision, exposing vastly disarticulated internal parts which flopped wetly on the sand. I was particularly chagrined because I didn't have my *bag of tricks* prop "hand" with me to insert into the incised stomach cavity— a rare photo op lost.

Someone (maybe it was me) mentioned that shark fillets were tasty and nutritious, and since we had a couple hundred pounds or so in front of us, Tim appropriately slashed and sawed (the not-so-keen edge of the Spyder-Co blade was not fairing well against the abrasive shark skin) off enough meat to feed us and half the population of Kitty Hawk. Just then, a back hoe trundled on the scene to sanitarily and summarily dispose the remainder of the somewhat abused carcass in a sandy grave—very appropriate for the shark and us; the beach dudes approved. The shark fillets were tastily marinated, cooked and consumed that evening by almost everyone. Those few not into oral adventure headed for MacDonalds.

The next day was spent at Kitty Hawk Kites messing around in the dunes and later, for the few who chose to, role playing "human lawn darts." The world's largest turn-stile school of hang gliding presented their programmed thrills, as we stumble/glided down low-angled dune slopes and implanted ourselves in the forgiving sand flat area below. This was *not* an exciting experience. Most of the now spectating group had decided not to submit themselves to the tedium of waiting interminably for a five-second glide; it was a wise decision.

Later on, we jumped and tumbled down a few more dunes and watched a surprisingly dull exhibition of stunt kite flying. (How come the bigger and louder kites always seem to be controlled by jerks? It's almost a given that someone flying an expensive, loudly flapping kite will be obnoxiously proud of how close they can come to your head and how much noise they can make—also near your head.

Everyone (I think) was looking forward to the next day when we were scheduled to tandem hang glide with an experienced pilot, who supposedly ran his business at the beach, and apparently out of the back of a truck. Hmmm . . .

The day dawned blustery, overcast, and cool; a complete contrast to the two previous near perfect days of 80 degrees and zephyr-like breezes. I mentally dismissed the beach-side rendezvous, as the wind was now gusting to 30 knots, but the adventurous spirit of the previously frustrated nouveau pilots renewed the contract with a phone call and found out that the flight was on; our beach-side pilot said, "Come on down!"

We drove the 45 minutes north to Currituck Beach and literally to the end of the road where, sure enough, Greg (our barnstorming pilot) was waiting with his glider seemingly affixed to the top of a small Toyota pick up. Considering the day, his outdoor office, and the memory of *human lawn darting* at Kitty Hawk, we asked for a demo flight (actually the group asked for a demo, because I was still sitting in the van reading [engrossed in a book by Edward Abbey, one of my favorite dead curmudgeons] convinced that it was too windy to fly safely, and considering the wind chill, too cold for comfort—my comfort.)

Greg's demonstration flight was apparently boffo, 'cause here comes one of the group to fetch me from the van; " . . . and they need eight people to sign up to get a ten-dollar-off deal, and it looks great, and he's very impressive, and Karl, you're number eight." And as it turned out he was, and I was, so I did—sign up I mean. For the next five hours we queued up to pay our reduced fee, get towed to 1,800 ft., glided about with Greg at the controls in a tandem set up, and eventually landed gently, effortlessly, and impressively within feet of where we began the flight.

Greg dutifully covered the basic flight and safety instructions with each individual rider, making sure that each passenger knew exactly what was going to happen and how he expected them to react in case of an emergency. The briefed and wide-eyed rider then stepped into his/her hang harness and suspended themselves with a carabiner from the glider's tubular fuselage. Greg and the rider were essentially flying suspended side by side, but most of the time the rider stabilized his/her position by looping an arm around the pilot's back and under his arm.

As the tow truck, which we were attached to the top of, picked up speed, Greg pulled a release pin and the air-craft abruptly became part of its element; the first 50 foot gain in elevation couldn't have taken more than three seconds. An altimeter, located directly next to my head, ticked off the altitude gain faster than I could count. When we

103

reached three hundred feet it looked like 1,000, and at our maximum height gain of 1,800 feet, I expected to hear a stewardess ask me what I wanted to drink.

As we continued being towed and gaining height, Greg pointed out different geographical points, also conversationally hinting at some of the intricacies of flight. I suspect this patter was partly to help me relax and also to break the silence, 'cause I wasn't saying much. I was hugely interested in the suddenly fragile-looking wing and skimpy cable connectors. I remembered Greg saying before we took off, that the glider had a shotgun shell activated ballistic parachute that could fully open in 1.5 secs. This second chance potential made me feel considerably more confident about touching down at less than 125 mph. (By the way, did you know that the world's fastest animal is a cow, dropped out of a helicopter? Pilot humor!)

We stayed at 1,800 feet for a few minutes just looking around, then Greg "cut loose" the tow line. It was interesting to watch the nylon rope fall and snake down toward the ground, until it just disappeared.

We glided in looping circles and large figure eights. Fear essentially disappeared as Greg's seductively smooth flying style tempted me to try the controls and experience flying beyond the goals I had set for myself. This was *really* hang gliding; nothing like the previous day's launch and land scenario.

As we gradually lost altitude and began heading back toward the beach landing area, my confident and skilled pilot asked if I would like to experience some acrobatics with him. I knew this was coming because the riders preceding this flight had encouraged me to say yes when he asked, and I did, but before the s was out of yes, Greg had us in a wing over and I was standing on my head looking straight down; not for long, as the continuation of the swooping maneuver threw us up and over to the other side and down, down, down . . . After a couple of those whoop-de-doos, I realized what an excellent pilot we had accidentally chosen.

If you have ever seen a sea gull or pelican landing into the wind, perhaps you can conjure a hologram of what our approach and touch-down looked like. Greg prided himself in gentle tandem landings; I don't think a sea gull could have done it better.

Considering myself somewhat of a connoisseur of paid for cheap thrills, I'd have to say this was the best. Greg was an excellent teacher, guide, and instructor—telling us what we needed to know, and not telling us what we didn't want to hear. Our 10–12 minutes of flight was not a Disneyland type of carnival ride, this was genuine bird-like gliding.

After the last flight we applauded and hugged our host (he initiated the hugs, part of the deal, I guess) and promised a return next year with more people.

Just about that time, a few of the folks from the Kitty Hawk kite festival showed up for the power kiting event. We had been operating on a quarter-mile-wide and ten-mile-long stretch of beach, but the power jerks wanted to set up their kites directly in the path of Greg's landing approach. Remember, these are not kids' kites, a Force 10 kite could easily foul the controls or rip the wing surface of a hang glider causing predictably tragic results. As we left, I noticed Greg asking them politely to set up their competition venue somewhat downwind of the area he had been using all morning. We were too far away to hear what was being said, but the power kiter's expressions were not happy, further justifying my opinion of people who fly big kites. If you ever buy a large kite, resist the kite's power to metamorphose your pleasant personality into a *surlyjerk—an aberrant neurosis I just made up for the occasion.*

CHAPTER 17

Bottom Line Dune Jumping

"It seems paradoxical that although most people love having fun and enjoy humor, that they are often resistant to its use. Perhaps the greatest resistance by people to the use of humor is the ingrained sense that work is work and play is play. Humor and fun suggest a lack of focus, a misuse of time, immaturity, and a lack of attention to what is really important ."

Napier/Gershenfield

107

ast week I was driving down (actually *up*) to Crane's Beach with a car full of Project Adventure staff members. We were doing our lunch hour (+30 minutes) exercise thing, heading for Massachusetts big-sky-country-at-the-beach and a run by the shore or in the dunes.

There's something therapeutically attractive to me about the stark geography of a beach scene, and I suspect it results from living within the heavily-forested East coast biome, and/or densely populated North Shore suburban area. Crane's Beach during the off season is rarely visited, so the excess people problem is nonexistent, and on a clear day you can imaginatively see beyond the blue curve all the way to Ireland. Eastern "big sky" country; it's worth the nine-mile drive.

There is something also mildly therapeutic about spending 30 minutes with five people in a Honda Civic. The conversation is inclusive, like it or not, and the feeling of camaraderie that develops from escaping the 9–5 milieu and sharing a physical adventure, lends itself to smiles and social sharing that otherwise would not take place.

The anticipation of this "break" reminds me of the current magazine articles I've read that emphasize the positive corporate aspects of experiencing fun in the workplace, including humor as part of your workday, and further recognizing the need for *serious* play toward achieving a flow state that balances uninhibited fun and a responsible work ethic. Although it's easy to make occupational fun of seeking occupational *funn,** (hard-core fun-sponges still equate play with sloth), I agree with the various article-authors above, because I've attempted over the years to live the theme (balancing the joys of occupational pursuits and play), and it works for me.

So there we drove and sat, elbow to elbow, trying to peer out the steamy windows and say something interesting, perhaps even witty, but also attempting to avoid the obvious social gaffes that five-in-a-Civic can engender. But the feel-good magic begins, enhanced by removal from the office scene, and doing something good for yourself with like-minded jolly companions *on company time.*

On arrival at the beach, with spirits and physical anticipation high, an unspoken question precedes the shedding of shoes and clothes, "What's the challenge today?" Sand sliding? A cold water dip? Kite fighting? A dash through the sand hills? Or maybe a jog to the shore break dunes in anticipation of a gripping fifteen foot vertical dune plunge. Happily, what we choose to do doesn't really matter, because the format is *funn* and doing is a given; unequivocal doing without the hassle of discussion, validation, or rationalization.

We head for the beach, each performing their own puppet-like warm-up ritual, conversationally sharing absolutely irrelevant topics of poignant interest. "The tide's in!" The tide's out! It's windy. It's cold. It's really hot. Did you bring your board? Shall I wear my shoes? Does photosynthetic potential in cold offshore water cause proliferation of red tide organisms?

After stretching, and a warm-up spate of retro-running (jogging backward), I announce, "I'm off for a short run through the sand hills, and I'll see you all at the steep shore break dunes in about twenty minutes."

The chopping, driving, running style in soft sand is considerably different from the longer, more fluid stride that results when running on a firm surface. Soft sand requires toe gripping, a shorter leg thrust, and a different mind set; you either learn to like it, or continue to hate it.

The "quad" sand trail takes me up, down, and around and across the constantly wind-changing dune scene. I revel in the familiar feelings of foot/sand contact, uphill soft-sand muscle chugging, and the consistent rediscovery of an animalistic urge to cause myself pain, the good pain that's indescribable to people of lesser physical passions.

The vertical dunes come quickly, and the 140 bpm carotid pulse I'm caressing lets me know I'm glad to be here. Zowie! Look what the storm has done for us! These sand hills have become literally half dunes, slashed and halved by the high tides and storm surf; massively eroded for our benefit, for our play.

The runner/players assemble quickly, each having completed their personal exercise goal, completely warmed up, ready for the challenge. Questions are asked, former dune jumps verbally compared, and exclamations made about vertical drop, impact, sand density, talus depth. Professional adventurers posturing atop the big dune; smiling, pumped, hesitant, gripped . . . and gone. Jumping again, further this time, and again, and again . . . This *is* funn!*

A giddy suggestion rises above the jumper's shouts. "Let's see if we can climb the vertical Half Dune." Scooped out holes for foot and hand soon pepper the 90 degree sand face, as 5.10 climbers (How do you rate a vertical sand dune?) try their ascent skills on a shifting medium. Some make it to the top, some don't, and no one cares. Great! Now let's see how fast an ascent can be made. Jumps and climbs,

---

*The word *funn* is an acronym for *functional understanding's not necessary.*

jumps and climbs and falling, over and over and over . . . This must be fun because there's no teams, no score, *no game*, and I'm feeling good. How come I'm smiling so much? Why are these crazy people so much fun to be with? What is the magic of these moments that makes life so sweet?

It's play, mate—pure play—play for the sake of being and doing. Spontaneous, uninhibited, hyper-reactive, no-reason fun.

Nearly spent, we jog the mile or so back to the main beach area. "How 'bout a dip?" It's November . . . are you nuts? "Yeah, let's go for it, and no fair running in, you have to wade out until the water slooowly covers your crotch." *Whhhaat?* The dip is consummated with wild yells, plunging bodies and toweled off promises of future deep winter dips.

The return trip steams the car windows, and is more subdued, but is also far richer in shared experience. The mood is mellow, the players primed and eager for whatever else the day has to offer. These five pumped individuals are not better people for having shared a physical adventure experience, but returning to the workplace they will likely rediscover a mental sharpness and vigor that was waning or perhaps, on this day, not there at all.

In 1986 a Project Adventure intern, Tom Del Prete, (now Dr. Del Prete) wrote a Christmas poem for me that's worth sharing. It is as follows:

Sand Dune Jumpers

Karl says people who jump down sand dunes
(you really can't jump off a sand dune)
Are special—no trophies, just joy and sand.

A few quick steps and then the leap,
Dig your heels in, smack your bottom down
or hurtle forward, and howl.

Rumi, the poet, in the 14th century,
   says Live,
Blake says the hills echo the little ones
   leaping and laughing;
Hopkins says amidst Victorian rectitude
   how about all this juice,
while Merton says from the monastery
   it is life that makes you dance.

These poet people kick up some sand,
their words jump down onto the page,
their words like Karl and cohorts
    springing down the dunes

Sand dune jumpers live otherwise;
their invitation is the sand alone,
their shadow their only following.

The wind dissolves all imprint of
the most emphatic landing;
The record of past jumps is in
the anticipation of the next.

Sand dune jumpers are special—
no trophies, just joy and sand.

The day after our Five-In-A-Civic trip to Crane's, Tom Zierk (a dune jumper of consummate skill himself) penned the following ditty:

Them Dune Jumpers

Lookit them dune jumpers
havin they funs
jumpin off sand dunes
landin on they buns

Lookit them dune jumpers
ain't they keen
lookin out for green trucks
hopein they ain't seen

Listen them sand sliders
ain't they loud
hootin down them sand slopes
an gigglin on the ground

They runnin up and fallin down
they messin in the sand
they climbin up an laughin loud
no carein how they land

Lookit them dune jumpers
ain't they wild
jumpin off an floatin down
they feelin likes a child

111

CHAPTER 18

Monkey Business

"One could do worse than be a swinger of birches."
Robert Frost

1984: I was building indoor challenge ropes courses in Pittsburgh for Project Adventure, during which time I received a message at the hotel from an old shark hunting buddy, John Herbert. Soon after those days of dipping in the bloody brine, (See *O Positive Chum* in this book.) John had landed a job cataloging primates in Africa and had, over the last 20 years, traveled throughout the African continent establishing game preserves, and enjoying an enviable lifestyle in the bush. Now he was back in the U.S. and eager to find a job that would adapt to his peripatetic lifestyle, provide some excitement, and pay a few bills.

After a day's dusty, dirty work hammer-drilling school gymnasium walls, in pursuit of the perfect faux climbing wall, I was looking forward to seeing John and having a beer, and considering the dust and grime lining my lips, not necessarily in that order. John had brought along a buddy of his, Mike, who shared a passion for exotic animals and full bore living. In good fellowship, we embellished some recent stories about our lives, laughing and joshing each other as old friends are apt to do, but as the conversation slowed, the two looked at each other indicating that the real reason for this get-together was about to be broached. John asked abruptly, "Did I want to join him and Mike on a small island off the coast of Puerto Rico as part of a primate relocation project for the U.S. Fish and Wildlife Department?" *Does a chicken have lips? Does Big Ben have ticks? Did I want to spend some time on a tropical uninhabited island chasing monkeys?*

Working for Project Adventure has provided some unique benefits over the years, one of which is a working style that offers occupational excitement and variety. However, when you get some of something, it's almost inevitable that you want more, and I did. The idea of living on a tropical island, trapping monkeys, and playing the role of not-so-great white hunter, switched off whatever responsibility I had to home and hearth. Karl, can-you-come-out-to-play? You bet! Wait for me guys! I couldn't remember being so excited about going somewhere for years.

As we sat there munching on HoJo goodies, John and Mike further increased my anticipation by filling me in on some island details. The name of the island was *Desecheo*, derived from the Spanish verb desechar: *to throw away*. This precipitous one mile by half mile chunk of desolate igneous outcropping was covered by scrub growth, cactus, Gumbo Limbo trees, and a plant that produced sticky seeds which clung tenaciously to leg hair. The island's circumference shore line was made up of jagged wave battered rocks, precluding any type of large boat landing.

Island inhabitants included an undetermined amount of Rhesus Macac monkeys (Macaca mulatta), feral goats and cats, a rookery of cohabiting Booby and Frigate birds, and an astronomical number of lizards and hermit crabs. Twenty meters from the shore there wasn't a natural flat place on the island, and there was no water except that which collected in rotted trees and rocky depressions after a rain. To top off this list of Club Med attractions, the island had been used extensively for aerial target practice and bombing runs during the Second World War, some of which ordnance, we were warned, *remained unexploded*. Desecheo, eleven miles off the western tip of Puerto Rico, was indeed a *throw away* island.

Leaving for Desecheo wasn't scheduled for a couple months, but it was all I could think about. During those weeks, I did best what any creative adventurer does, I dreamed of and embellished every fine imagined scenario to come, planned for every practical and imagined contingency, and in the process became conceptually acclimated to the island. All this prime time day dreaming did not put me in the running for father/husband of the year.

Ostensibly I was being hired as the expedition photographer. John had posed the question at HoJo's if that role suited me. After I had enthusiastically answered yes, he further asked, "You do have a camera, don't you?" I had no doubt in my mind at that point, that this was a serious expedition being undertaken by three big kids.

The scientific rationale for the expedition was to rid the island of monkeys via live trapping, and later transport the humanoid rascals to the Mayaguez Zoo on the mainland of Puerto Rico. The Fish and Wildlife people were convinced that these prehensile primate raiders, not finding much else palatable on the island, had developed a taste for eggs. It had been noticed by more than one visiting scientist that the previously large numbers of roosting Booby and Frigate birds on Desecheo had been dramatically diminished. There was absolutely no evidence for the assumption that the monkeys were at fault, but monkeys like eggs, right? The monkeys were, of course, immediately blamed, and condemned to capture. Some Macacs would be placed in the zoo as previously mentioned, and some would be used for medical research, but what exotic research. . . Oooh La La!

Apparently, among the academic community at Mayaguez, a certain bodily function of the female Macac was of consuming interest. So much so, that one of the doctoral researchers wrote for and received a substantial grant that would allow him to determine if the female Macac (Are you ready for this?) *was capable of orgasm.* It's True. This risque research was worth a few ongoing smiles amongst the three island hunters, but to be honest, I never did find out what the study determined, or how they were planning on conducting the tests. I do remember that the first six monkeys we trapped and helicoptered to the mainland were males, which led to inevitable jokes about a gay monkey population . . . Hunter's humor.

The Rhesus monkeys inhabiting Desecheo at that time were the progeny of an original batch that had been placed on the island about twenty years earlier by a scientific group that was interested in utilizing the introduced colony as an animal breeding pool for medical research. A 100′ X 100′ concrete helipad, still in excellent condition, had been constructed near the shore so that helicopters could land and ferry monkeys back to the mainland. I'm not sure why they thought the island-acclimated monks would come running and hop on the occasional chopper, but they didn't, and the experiment was eventually abandoned, as were the monkeys. Since there was no natural source of water on the island, the instigators of this initial incestuous breeding scheme probably thought the poor primates would eventually die off; a medical setback and financial disaster of six figure proportion, but after all, it *was* the monkey's fault for not cooperating and coming when called.

Mike met me at the San Juan airport, the termination of my flight from frigidly cold Boston. I had left in the snow to arrive at this 80 degree tropical destination; I was feeling good. Mike had lived in Puerto Rico previously, working as the curator of the Mayaguez Zoo, so his knowledge of the island and the language was well beyond what remained of my sometime academic involvement with Spanish 101. We headed for the airport bar and a cool *cerveza* to wait for John's plane. I couldn't help but fantasize that this was a movie set, and I was an actor in a National Geographic special.

John arrived within the hour, looking *old*. He had come down with a raging case of the flu, but had refused to stay home. (He later admitted his reason for not staying home was that he was determined

---

*On page 185–186 of the book, Why Things Are, by Joel Achenbach, (Copyright 1991), I quote, "We do know that female primates, such as Rhesus monkeys, can be manipulated to orgasm in a laboratory." So you see, this important research (1985) has already impacted the academic world. Perhaps not in a profound way, but, hey...we can't all make the big time.

not to let us have all the fun.) As the next two weeks of mainland-based activities transpired, I had to give John credit for functioning at any level when it was obvious that he was not at all well. But he did begin to improve, and I have to believe that he was better off at 80+ degrees in Puerto Rico, than the sub freezing temperatures and deep snow he left behind in Ohio.

During our mainland based time we procured food, had traps made, collected oranges and bananas for bait, and arranged for helicopter transportation. We spent most of this mainland time based at the Wildlife Refuge station near Cabo Rojo. The Refuge, our temporary home and The Caribbean Fish and Wildlife center, had at one time been a CIA world-wide radio listening post, a audial spy center, so to speak. It's hard to imagine, but as you entered The Refuge area you drove beneath a double overlapping grid of cables that formed an overhead bowl shaped radio receiver, much like the one at Arecibo, but considerably smaller.

To engineer this double-grid cable net, huge wooden utility poles had been sunk vertically in a large diameter circle, (diameter of approx. 700 ft.) and cross circle cables had been connected from pole top to pole top to form the two tautly strung wire grids that were suspended 12" apart (top to bottom) and were made up of 12" X 12" grid squares. Each of the 20+ utility poles measured over 100 feet high, and were so massive in girth that it took two people to encircle the base with their arms. To someone who builds ropes courses for a living, this was truly the Parthenon of challenge courses. The entire area was an engineering marvel, and it had been abandoned for over 10 years.

After we had been there for a few days, and during some down time, I couldn't resist climbing one of the poles. I didn't think I would ever see utility poles that large again so, pulling myself up to the first pole-step, I climbed the regularly placed steel rods unbelayed (no protection rope) to the top. I don't remember much about the view, but I do recall the frightening perspective as I looked down past my toes, and also wondering why I was there.

Later that day, still pumped with adrenaline (adventure juice) from the pole climb, I pulled myself up, through, and onto the overhead cable grid from the top of one of the buildings and, standing erect on the grid itself, wondered what would happen to a skydiver who inadvertently tried to land on the area covered by this giant cheese slicer. As far as I know, the cable grid is probably still there because no one would commit to take it down for fear of damaging the buildings underneath.

Soon thereafter, with all our preparations complete, a Coast Guard helicopter took us out to Desecheo. As we approached what appeared

117

to be a desolate speck of land, I heard one of the crew say, "I can't believe you guys are going to spend a month on death island." *Death Island?* Before I could ask, we were there, circling the deeply-eroded topography, trying desperately to mentally record surface features for future on-foot reference.

Since we planned to use oranges as monkey bait for the traps, and since the island-bound primates had never seen or smelled an orange, we asked the pilot if he would continue circling at a lower altitude so we could bomb the island with a couple hundred oranges, hoping that the smell of impact exploded citrus would attract the monks and initiate an instantly acquired taste. Our thinking was, if there's no water, oranges are going to smell and taste awfully good: perfect bait material.

The "bombing runs" were performed in true military fashion. The captain said that since we were civilians we could not be involved in such a blatant militaristic undertaking, so the crew would have to drop the oranges; an obviously shallow attempt to keep us from having fun. With the captain maintaining a running commentary over the intercom and zooming around the island at about 200 feet, the crew dispatched their bomb load with gusto. I don't know what the monkeys thought of the cascading orange pellets, but it was damned exciting in the helicopter.

Securing from combat mode, the captain set down easily on the heli pad. With some help from the crew we unloaded our gear quickly, and without any hesitation the chopper took off. The captain related that he had to account for his flying time, and the orange bombing caper had eaten into his allotted flight time. "Have a good time mates, see you next week." The helicopter was scheduled to return in five days to bring supplies (mostly water) and ferry back any captured monkeys. We had no radio contact with the mainland, so we were suddenly and unequivocally on our own.

John and Mike had been to the island five years earlier during a previous monkey hunting expedition, so they knew where to arrange camp, set the traps, bathe in the surf, defecate, etc., so I followed their lead...most of the time. In a short time it looked like we had been there for days, and with a few hours of light remaining we went on a hike to check out the results of our various "bomb" runs, and to get a feel for the territory.

During that walk we only saw one smooshed orange, which either meant that the monkeys loved oranges or we spread the oranges too thin for the geography. Also during that time I was introduced to the male Rhesus Macac.

We hiked along the coral strewn shore for a few hundred yards, eventually turning inland toward the dense undergrowth. John remembered a location nearby that had been a popular feeding spot, but the years of tropical growth had almost completely obliterated the trail. From the air, this area had looked like a soft green carpet, but now beneath the aerial carpet we hacked with machetes through thick undergrowth, thankful that no species of snake had ever been identified on Desecheo, but wondering what 45 years of sun and humidity would do to a live bomb. Our discomfort was short-lived, as we broke into a clearing that was familiar to our leader. John's sense of direction and recollection was dead on, as we practically fell over an old trap.

John and Mike closely inspected the two traps to see if any part of the release mechanisms still worked. The traps were made of aluminum tubing, which welded tubes supported heavy duty rabbit wire as a covering. They measured approximately 3" X 3' X 5' and were so constructed that they could be folded flat to facilitate transportation. The traps were high tech, the trap release wasn't. As a monkey entered the open end of the trap, he/she was enticed by an orange, banana, or dry kibbled monkey food, which bait was tied to the trip lever of a common rat trap. When the rat trap was sprung, the swiftly moving rectangular trap bar jerked an attached thin wire that was distantly attached to a dead bolt that held the sliding trap door open. The resulting pull-this/jerk-that sequence, was a swiftly closing trap door and a very disgruntled monkey. The traps were large enough to allow us to crawl inside in order to check the rat trap mechanism, resulting in a *photo op* of rare design.

As the work continued, John quietly mentioned that there was a large male Macac watching us from the edge of the clearing. In my ignorance, I looked immediately in that direction, then directly at the monkey. Recognizing my oafish stare as a sign of obvious aggressiveness, the Macac jutted his head forward, jumped up and down a couple times, emitted a staccato hooting sound, then split so fast it was hard to imagine that he had been there at all. *OK, so don't use me for bait.* I had a lot to learn about primate animal behavior, including my own.

During one of those early reconnaissance trips on the island, as the three of us were struggling through a rock strewn gully, we practically tripped over a large unexploded bomb. The bomb measured about three feel long, and except for the missing stabilizing fins, which had rusted off, looked just like what you would expect a World War 11 bomb to look like.

After hastily retreating, we pussyfooted around the area, sneaking closer and closer for a better look, and eventually taking one another's picture next to the egg-like casing. We never touched the rusted metal, but I have to admit, it was foolishly exciting just being in the area. The entire sequence, from surprised discovery to our hesitating reapproach of the area, was as if scripted for a Monty Python skit.

John had his scoped rifle with him, and we seriously considered taking a few shots at the bomb from two or three hundred yards away; as a service to the Fish and Wildlife folks, of course. Well...we never did for a number of reasons.

- We thought that a bomb that size going off would attract some attention from the mainland and would cause the Coast Guard to think that we had blown ourselves up.
- We didn't want to spook the monkeys frequenting the area.
- We needed the time to continue our reconnaissance.
- Thinking about setting off a bomb that big scared the hell out of us.

We stumbled on a couple other smaller pieces of unexploded ordnance during the time we were there, and saw many pounds of exploded metal while tramping the ridges and valleys. After awhile we paid little attention to any of it, as it became just another part of Desecheo's hard-line charm.

The next few days were taken up with establishing a living routine at the helipad and placing the traps. Since the traps were foldable, we hiked them to many of their final locations on ridges and valleys, an arduous task at best considering the thick, prickly vegetation and the steep angle of the hills. (Remember, this island went from sea level [helipad] to 700 feet within half a mile: that's goat country!).

We still had not moved some of the traps to the more remote locations by the end of the week when the Coast Guard flyboys returned. They were obviously disappointed that we had not trapped any monkeys yet (so were we), and asked if they could be of any help, probably anticipating another orange bomb run scenario. We asked if they could airlift a few of our folded traps to the highest ridges. They had the time, sure . . . load them on—and we did.

Probably because I was the only person who had rock climbing experience, I was chosen to accompany the traps out the helicopter door. The nonchalant crew members of the helicopter asked me if I had ever descended from a chopper using an underarm yoke. I answered honestly no, but the entire truth was that this was only the second time I had ever been in a helicopter. They said it was easy, then slipped a padded nylon loop that looked like a horse's collar over my head and under my arms. I think I remember them telling me to keep my arms down, and the next thing I knew the crane boom swung me away from the fuselage so that I was looking 100 ft. down past my toes. (I'm convinced that looking down from 1,000 feet is easier than looking down from 100. There's little perspective from 1,000 feet that you can relate to, but the view from 100 feet is just enough to set off any number of survival receptors.) Almost immediately the winch began lowering me smoothly toward the hill top. The nice thing about the yoke set-up was that when I touched the ground I could immediately step out of the yoke and not get dragged about or jerked back up into the air. I was on the ground, disengaged, and signaling them to reverse the winch.

Not surprisingly, it takes a considerable amount of prop-thrusted wind to support a multi-ton aircraft. I knew there was going to be some wind from the props as I descended, but not THAT much. As the pilot maintained his hover position, the crew prepared the traps for lowering. The down draft was unbelievable. I was being battered with at least a 100-mile-an-hour wind that was hitting me directly from above, in addition to getting pelted with every loose piece of vegetation within 50 feet. I was no longer enjoying my envied role of helicopter trap monitor.

The crew had some trouble getting the traps out the aircraft door, but once free of the chopper they descended smoothly. All I had to do was grab the cable and unclip the connecting carabiner. As the traps bounced up and down, I began to appreciate why hovering was not an exact locational technique. I could see the crewman above yelling toward me, and I'm sure they were berating me for not getting the traps undone with more dispatch, but the fact was I couldn't catch the darn things as they swayed from side to side, also bouncing up and down off the irregular terrain. I wasn't worried about my personal safety since I was on the ground and not attached, but I suddenly recognized why the crew was so agitated, as the traps drifted toward a copse of hilltop Gumbo Limbo trees. If that chicken-wire trap package got caught in the tree limbs, what would happen to the helicopter? (I found out later that they would have disengaged from above, but I didn't know that at the time.) Jumping on the bouncing traps like a cowboy on a grounded steer, I worked practically sightless under the vertical hurricane force wind, and somehow got the cable disengaged. The helicopter immediately banked to the right and disappeared over the ridge top, out of sight and sound. I remained perched on top of my trophy, amazed at the loud sound of my own heavy breathing, the oppressive heat, and the silence from above.

Not surprisingly, trap lowering wasn't attempted again. In the weeks to come, the choppers (Coast Guard, Army, Navy and civilian) ferried food and water to us and monkeys back to the mainland, period: the close call had come too close.

We developed a trapping routine as the days went by that involved early rising, exercise, setting and checking the traps, then waiting until the following day to repeat the procedure. To further our fitness fixation, John and I used the helipad as our early AM workout venue. Mike sensibly used this time to continue sleeping or continue eating, smiling tolerantly at our nude helipad follies. The walking, stretches, and lifting series of exercises were, of course, performed in the buff because the ambient temperature was just right, the blazing sun wasn't high enough to fry our buns, the monkeys didn't care and neither did we. I was becoming acclimated to the environment and to our simplistic way of living.

During our first few days on the island, the three of us had scrounged the rocky shore for whatever flotsam could be used to improve our domestic situation. We had tents for shelter, so our scrounging forays were more aimed at dragging back driftwood boards to be used for tables and shelves. The precipitous and jaggedly weathered coral shore offered no trails, so our ant-like trips back to camp laden with various sized boards were arduous, uncomfortable and dangerous. Type of wood, grain, and finish had little to do with which board was chosen for camp use. If it was the right size, it was the right board.

Our campsite next to the helipad became home. After spending a hot, water-rationed day in the hills, we all looked forward to that final stretch of rocky beach that announced water, shelter, food, and the camaraderie of shared stories. Life on Desecheo was simple. There was only so much that could be done, and our needs were few. The physical life kept us pleasantly hungry, and the exercise of tramping the hills provided a level of C-V fitness that Jane Fonda would have extolled.

John and Mike had brought weapons to the island. The Fish and Wildlife department had not only requested that we trap all the monkeys, but to also try and rid the island of any feral animals; i.e., wildlife not indigenous to the island. There was no chance of trapping goats, and cats were too small to remain trapped. So, as we made our trapping rounds, we began to carry rifles and shotguns. John and Mike had scoped .222 varmint bangers; high velocity, extremely accurate rifles. I carried a double barrelled 12 guage shotgun, which says it all about my aiming technique. We occasionally took the shots that needed to be taken, but even after we were finished on the island there were still goats and cats remaining. As long as the Puerto Ricans continued to dump their unwanted animals on the island, the feral problem will remain extant.

If you have never fired a 12 guage shotgun with a magnum load, it's hard to appreciate what the recoil is like, and even more difficult for me to explain. Suffice it to say that if you are a small person, there is a good chance that your person will join the recoil in a corporeal displacement that might end up with you on your backside. And, if you hold the rifle stock tentatively against your shoulder, the kick will surely bruise muscles, causing you to flinch on the next shot, and result in people saying, "I see why you need a shotgun."

It was exciting to approach a trap in anticipation of possibly seeing a monkey, but many traps were sprung and empty. After awhile, we determined that small birds were the scavenging culprits, and there wasn't much we could do to deter their bait-stealing except use bait that the monkeys liked and the birds didn't; unfortunately, the birds liked everything. But the occasional trapped monkey kept the work interesting.

The procedure for transporting a Rhesus from trap to helipad was well implemented by my two zoologically adept companions. John would attract the angry monkey's attention on one side of the cage, while Mike, tranquilizing syringe in hand, tried to grab the monk's tail through the trap. After much maneuvering, and with tail in hand, Mike pulled the monk's rump right up to the cage grid. The trick then was to quickly administer the needle to a howling, snarling, bucking Macac before he/she reached around and gave you the needle. The Ketamine tranquilizer quickly did its job, and the very upset primate took a 45-minute trip to La La Land. During this down time, John and Mike had a hurried opportunity to describe and record weight, teeth condition, parasite infestation (nonexistent on Desecheo monkeys), sex, approximate age and general condition, (always excellent—these monkeys were flat-out healthy and well acclimated to this liquidless environment. Where were they getting their food and water? Bird eggs? Things were starting to look bad for our prehensile defendants.)

Then it was time to hustle the beggars down to camp before the happy juice wore off. If they came to while tucked in the back packs, a hungover Macac would do more than tickle your ears. Have you ever seen an adult male Macac's incisors? Probably not, but they are considerably longer than yours, and well situated in a prognathous jaw to facilitate chomping whatever parts of your body that come too close.

Back at the helipad we transferred the monkeys into smaller transportation cages for the chopper ride back to the mainland. I don't know where they had tripped out on Ketamine (a hallucinogen), but when they came back, *happy* was not a descriptive adjective. At this snarling, head bashing stage, I wondered what techniques they had developed back on the mainland toward determining whether the female Macac was capable of orgasmic behavior. Every few days the helicopter would arrive and our furry, disgruntled helipad companions would leave.

As the days and weeks went by, we amused ourselves in various low tech ways. I gained a greater appreciation of how folks used to spend their evening hours before TV, radio, or even electricity. When the sun went down, darkness came quickly, and considering that the nearest theater, library, or pub, was a 15-mile boat ride away, we settled down in our tents for the evening's entertainment; reading. Many, many books were read and conversationally shared by kerosene lamp.

During the day we collected floating coconuts, sawed the nuts into bowls, and polished them with rocks and sand. Vying for the best looking dinner bowl or water cup occupied many hours of pleasant handy work. Parts of the island not visited for trap checks were explored for flotsam "beach treasures," and occasionally people from the mainland would visit for a few days. It was fun to show off the island, the geography of which we were very familiar with by this time.

Mary, a friend of Mike's who had worked with him at the Mayaguez Zoo, visited occasionally to check out the island primate situation, Macac and Sapiens. She and I had talked earlier on the mainland about doing some skin diving off the rock beach near the helipad, so on one of her visits she brought snorkeling gear for both of us. The water surrounding the island became deep very quickly, occasioning migrating whales to closely approach our rocky beach location. Many times during meals or recreation time on the helipad, our attention was drawn to the ocean by the sound of whale's exhaling; they were that close. Although we didn't anticipate seeing any whales while snorkeling, we knew the deeper water just off shore would tempt larger marine animals to cruise by in hopes of snaring a shallow water meal. This big-fish-eats-little-fish biological scenario was not exactly the stimulus I was looking for to enhance the experience, but we donned our gear on a beautifully warm day without trepidation and paddled off in search of salty adventure.

We used no wet suits, as the water near the surface was comfortably warm. We also carried no spear guns, just the basic mask, flippers, snorkel combination. It was exciting to swim just a few meters off shore and be looking down 40–60 feet through crystal clear water to the large boulders and rock formations that made up the broken bottom. Small brightly-hued tropical fish were abundant, with the occasional large green or blue parrot fish adding to the panoply of contrasting color.

It always takes me some time in order to emotionally acclimatize when I make the transition from beach to depth. I'm never immediately comfortable with that radical change in environment or different spatial perceptions that occur in deep clear water. Mary and I tagged after each other, peering and goose-necking this way and that into the deepening water, taking considerable comfort from the fact that there was another species of our kind nearby.

After about 15 minutes we had cruised into rather deep water (much beyond my free-diving limit). To my left, on the offshore side, I saw at the limit of my underwater vision a large stationary dark object about 6 feet below the surface. *It* was easily my size, even considering the magnification resulting from juxtaposing mask and water. Retreat sensors and adrenalin synapses had shifted my adventure quotient into the minus category, but *it* was just beyond framing, and I just had to see what *it* was. Without checking to locate Mary, and with my eyes filling the mask, I kicked twice toward the stationary object. **THAT'S ENOUGH—IT'S A BARRACUDA!—IT'S THE GUINESS BARRACUDA!** Up to that point, Mary and I had been pretty much side by side, going our separate ways tentatively and returning for the relative comfort that a fellow diver provides. When I recognized what *it* was, I spun around, and saw Mary about ten feet behind looking at me quizzically. Gesticulating wildly and bubbly towards Mary, then toward shore, I abruptly decided to see how fast I could make my swim fins go up and down. I didn't stop kicking until the shore rocks began to grate against my chest, at which point I thought I should stop and make a gentlemanly gesture to see how Mary was doing. She was not far behind, smiling enormously at my obvious attempt to draw the cuda away from her with my wild kicking. I agreed, of course, that it was the least I could do.

When barracudas become old and large, they lose their characteristic silver color and become almost entirely black. *It* was pure **black**. Barracudas are known for being curious, and for being a ferocious game fish, but attacks on humans are practically non-existent. However, I never have depended much on statistics, and it was sooo **big!**

Having been ostensibly hired as the expedition photographer, I had two cameras with me and a plethora of film. And since I was trying to do a documentary of the entire expedition process, it was, of course, important to get photos of those things peripheral to the trapping process itself. The diminishing of the indigenous bird population had brought us here, so it was obviously imperative to get some close-ups of both the endangered Booby and Frigate birds. These birds rested and bred on the island, but spent most of the day far off shore fishing. Their late afternoon return each day was predictable, and if

125

the sun and clouds were just right, also occurred during perfect Galen Rowell, diffused God-light photographic time.

Because of the accumulation of guano, you could easily determine where the birds were nesting from our campsite location. I headed off one afternoon in that direction to photographically immortalize the birds whose eggs were supposedly being devoured by the monkeys. John came with me to help with the technical aspects, which I couldn't specify or generalize, but it was nice to have someone along.

We spent at least an hour moving carefully above the roost, trying our best to be ultra-quiet, which was difficult, considering that an insidious plant seed had attached itself in untold numbers to the hairs on my bare legs. My legs were covered, sock tops to shorts, to the extent that it looked like I was wearing a pair of fuzzy pants. These seeds were large and tenacious, each requiring a painful commitment to remove. That evening as I plucked off the seeds, with a separate ouch for every one, I purposefully placed each hairy seed (mostly *my* hair) in the campfire. I refused to be a willing carrier for such an effective biological dispersal scheme.

Eventually we achieved a near perfect location. With my longest (300 mm) lens, I framed a nesting Booby perfectly against the out-of-focus blue of the ocean backdrop; I was ecstatic. I shot off a roll of color slide film and was changing to some print film when John asked if I wanted to get closer. We were then about 75 feet away from the subject and I couldn't imagine achieving a better position without frightening the birds, but I agreed.

John casually walked right up to the birds and stood there waiting for me. I couldn't believe it. I had shot a whole roll of film with a long lens, and there he stood close enough to pet the damn things. Disgruntled, I joined him, and with a normal lens finished off the roll. The clincher was when I asked him how we could have gotten so close without spooking the birds. His answer said it all. "That's why they call them boobys."

Bathing at the beach was easy; slap on some Palmolive liquid soap (it lathers in salt water) scrub-a-dub-dub and plunge into the ocean, or more civilly take your daily ablutions in a tide pool, a nicely proportioned bathing area that was flushed every thirty seconds or so. I remember lying in a shallow tide pool, enjoying the warm air and water, and having a small octopus slither out onto my foot: ah, the stimuli of adventure baths.

One afternoon, after spending a long sweaty day trapping in the hills, John and I headed for the big salt bath for a scrub and dip. We were well lathered with Palmolive when I noticed two people walking toward us over the high tide reef. I rinsed off and grabbed a pair of shorts, because the two distant figures had a distinctly female walk.

John is one of the fastest eaters I have ever been around (a positive natural selection survival trait), but he takes forever while in the shower, or in this case, the ocean. With John in the buff so to speak, it was obviously my responsibility to act as welcoming committee. The two young, very brown, and not unattractive women rattled off a string of Spanish that I caught only the first word of, "Hola!------------------------". My limited Spanish vocabulary was used up in the first 15 seconds, so I shouted to Mike for assistance. Here comes Mike with a rifle, and I'm wondering why he's still carrying a weapon; he's not smiling.

After a few minutes of unintelligible chatter, Mike tells me that these women are two of twenty people that have illegally travelled from the Dominican Republic to try and start a new life in Puerto Rico. The twenty Dominicano aliens had made the 85-mile open ocean crossing in a 22' Boston Whaler (with only 6" of freeboard), and because of head winds and contrary seas were out of food and water. Food was not a concern apparently, but they had over 20 miles to go and the group had been parched by the tropical sun, and without water for many hours. The two women offered to stay with us for the night if we would give them water for the group. Mike seems agitated, and John is uncharacteristically aloof. I think, what the heck, invite the group over and let them drink their fill, we have more than enough. Before we can make any decision, here come the other 18 travellers, and they are *all* men. John whispers to me to get the shotgun and keep it near. I still haven't caught on to what's happening.

The men are all very dark-skinned, with little clothing, but almost each one has a large sheath knife hanging from a belt. They don't say much, except furitively to one another, but carefully eye our stores, water, and the guns. There is a desperateness about them that is palpable and very disconcerting; frightening. The three of us stand, weapons in hand, as if waiting for guests at a ludicrous cocktail party. Mike continues talking to a couple of them and offers water. They eagerly fill their carried containers from our 5 gallon gerry cans. Suddenly the conversation becomes more animated, and Mike steps back toward John and me as the group hastily finishes filling their bottles, spilling more than they capture. They all leave in haste, chattering to one another as if pursued by an imagined enemy.

We asked Mike what had spooked them. He told them we had a ship-to-shore transmitter and were obliged to make radio contact with the Coast Guard each afternoon at just about this time, also that if the CG didn't hear from us they would send a helicopter out to make a visual check. Since entering Puerto Rico as aliens was highly illegal, the Dominicanos were off to their boat for a quick get-away.

Our fight or flight hormonal centers were still pumping out copious amounts of adrenalin. We all agreed that Mike's fast thinking (we *had* no radio) might have saved our lives. Those twenty refugees were obviously very desperate people, and even though they were gone, I was not convinced that they were really gone. What was to keep them from going around to the other side of the island, swimming ashore, and doing us in after dark? We were really hyper now, so each of us took turns patrolling the helipad after the sun went down. As I patrolled back and forth on the 100' concrete square, both barrels of the shotgun loaded with #6 shot, I wondered if I could have brought myself to fire this devastating weapon at a group of humans. I fantasized many grisly scenarios about the afternoon encounter, and also about how I would react right then if attacked.

As the night wore on, our fears decreased to the point that we decided to get in our tents for some sleep. I told both Mike and John that if they had any intentions of getting a drink before sun-up (the water cans were next to my tent), they had better make a lot of noise, because the ole double guage was sleeping with me this night.

I don't know if that group of Dominicanos ever reached the mainland of Puerto Rico, but I would guess that they did. If they had not, the channel sharks would have eliminated all human evidence of their flight for freedom. That type of commitment is hard for a middle-class American to understand, and I had to respect them for taking such a huge chance in crossing their personal Rubicon toward what they thought would be a better life.

Toward the end of our first tour on the island, we were asked by the Wildlife folks to perform autopsies on a few of the monkeys to check their stomach contents and determine if they were indeed gobbling eggs. We shot a few of the older male Macacs that were avoiding the traps, and found that their stomach contents consisted almost entirely of Gumbo Limbo vegetation (the indigenous and most frequently found tree on the island). These monkeys had been relocated to a very harsh and waterless environment, and had apparently adapted beautifully to a largely vegetarian diet. What caused a reduction in the Booby and Frigate avian population was probably a combination of different environmental pressures; people on the island poaching eggs, poor eggshell consistency, reduction in food supply, etc. Maybe the monkeys did harass the birds as a diversion; God knows there's not much else to do on the island.

Each warm cloudless day eased into the next as we finished up our sixth week on Desecheo. I dreaded the day of my departure because I was ending an idyllic portion of my life, and knew that my two island comrades were remaining to continue the trapping operations. When the time demanded, I reluctantly helicoptered to San Juan to catch a plane back to Boston. The inevitability of being a serious person/parent/employee was once again upon me.

During the trans-Puerto Rico chopper flight, my pilot asked me if I had ever flown through a rainbow. Of course I hadn't, so he headed for one of the local showers that could be seen intermittently wetting the lush countryside. As we flew into a misty curtain, the sun's prismatic display circled the aircraft so that everywhere you looked there was color. We were literally in the center of a circular rainbow—extraordinary! (Which also reminds me; during the time that we spent at the Refuge, prior to leaving for Desecheo, one evening I walked outside during the full moon and was surprised by seeing a colorless rainbow, the arc of which was represented only in shades of gray. The moon was so bright that its light produced a monochromatic representation of a rainbow as a local shower passed by.)

Mike and John stayed on for another two months, but eventually also had to "get back to work". Their sun-drenched letters about monkeys, lung-burning hikes, and helipad humor made me long to be back on the island, and I wondered if I ever would ever again revisit Desecheo.

An inspection by Fish and Wildlife personnel a few weeks after the Mike and John left, indicated that the monkey population had been greatly reduced, but that there was *at least* one mating pair left. The monkeys had won this round.

Unbelievably, a year later we were back as a team (because of the then popular movie *Ghost Busters*, we called ourselves The Monkey Busters), and this time John and I brought our families out to the island for the ten days surrounding Christmas, but that's another story. What a joy to wake up Christmas morning and not have to listen to Alvin and the Chipmunks sing or hear *Feliz Navidad* ad nauseum. Our Christmas tree consisted of a delicate cactus skeleton decorated with red and green shotgun shells—very appropriate and definitely de rigueur among Desecheo's elite social community.

On the last day of the families' visit, and the day when we were all returning home, I walked the Desecheo valleys and ridges with my wife and two boys. I wanted to share with them some of the areas that I had become so familiar with, and pay my respects to the memory of a transplanted primate band that made the mistake of adapting too successfully. We put in some hard walking and climbing that day, eventually ending up on the highest ridge, allowing us to look toward the far southern end of the island; a place that I had seldom visited because of the rough terrain and dense undergrowth. The overhead sun, intensely brilliantly in a cloudless sky, allowed unlimited visibility.

My wife, Gloree, said, "What are those small animals over there (pointing south toward a lower ridge), aren't they monkeys?" My immediate and honest response was, "No, they're all gone. We haven't seen a sign of monkeys in almost ten days." As I raised my binoculars to check out the small but familiar objects, I instinctively knew what they were. "It's a band of nine monkeys," I intoned. We looked at each other, and she smiled. I grimaced.

What the hell . . .!

Karl Rohnke is one of the founders of Project Adventure, Inc., and currently serves as the president of that company. He often lives in Wenham, Massachusetts with his wife Gloree and two sons Matthew and Drew.

Other adventure curriculum books to his credit include:

- Cowstails and Cobras II
- Silver Bullets
- The Bottomless Bag & the Bottomless Baggie
- Forget Me Knots

Write to or call Kendall/Hunt Publishing Company for information about obtaining these books.

Kendall/Hunt Publishing Company
2460 Kerper Boulevard
P.O. Box 539
Dubuque, IA 52004–0539

(800) 228–0810